HOW TO LAUNCH
A SUCCESSFUL KICKSTARTER CAMPAIGN

CRAIG SOLACE

Contents

Introduction

Launching a successful Kickstarter campaign is no small feat, but with the right planning, preparation, and promotion, you can make it happen. This book will walk you through every step from conceptualizing your project, setting a realistic funding goal and reward tiers, creating compelling video and images, building your backer community, and running a successful campaign.

Who Should Read This Book?

- Entrepreneurs launching a new product or business.

- Creatives seeking funding for artistic projects.

- Innovators with a passion for bringing ideas to life.

- Anyone interested in understanding the nuances of successful crowdfunding.

I hope you'll join me on this journey - the first steps start here.

1 Understanding Kickstarter

In order to understand the rise of Kickstarter and its significance in the world of crowdfunding, it is important to trace back the roots of this phenomenon. Crowdfunding, as a concept, has been around for centuries, but it wasn't until recent years that it gained significant traction and popularity.

The earliest known form of crowdfunding can be traced back to the 18th century, when a subscription model was used to fund the publication of books. In this model, individuals would contribute a certain amount of money in exchange for a copy of the book once it was published. This approach allowed authors to finance the printing and distribution costs without relying on traditional publishers.

Fast forward to the late 20th century, and crowdfunding began to take shape in various industries. In the music industry, for example, musicians started using crowdfunding to raise funds for album production and distribution. They would offer exclusive rewards to their supporters, such as signed copies of the album or private concerts, in exchange for financial contributions.

The rise of the internet in the early 2000s brought crowdfunding to a whole new level. With the emergence of online platforms, it became easier than ever for individuals to connect with potential backers and promote their projects to a global audience. This shift opened up doors for entrepreneurs, artists, and creators of all kinds to seek funding for their ideas and bring them to life.

However, it wasn't until the launch of Kickstarter in 2009 that crowdfunding truly took off. Kickstarter revolutionized the crowdfunding landscape by offering a platform specifically designed for creative projects. The founders of Kickstarter, Perry Chen, Yancey Strickler, and Charles Adler, wanted to create a space where artists, musicians, filmmakers, and designers could showcase their ideas and gain support from a community of like-minded individuals.

Kickstarter introduced an "all-or-nothing" funding model, which means that project creators must set a funding goal and only receive the funds if they reach or exceed that goal within a specified timeframe. This model provided a level of security for backers, as they knew their contributions would only be used if the project had a real chance of success.

The success of Kickstarter in its early years sparked a crowdfunding revolution. Other platforms began to emerge, each with its own unique approach and target audience. Indiegogo, for example, focused on a more flexible funding model, allowing project creators to keep the funds raised even if they didn't reach their initial goal.

Today, crowdfunding has become a powerful tool for individuals and organizations across a wide range of industries. From creative projects to technological innovations, crowdfunding has enabled countless ideas to become a reality. It has democratized the funding process, allowing anyone with a compelling idea to seek support and turn their dreams into tangible projects.

Kickstarter: Leading the Revolution in Crowdfunding

When it comes to crowdfunding platforms, Kickstarter is a name that stands out from the crowd. Since its launch in 2009, Kickstarter has revolutionized the way people fund creative projects and business ventures. It has become a leader in the crowdfunding industry, inspiring countless other platforms to follow suit. So, what sets Kickstarter apart? Let's take a closer look at how this platform has led the revolution in crowdfunding.

One of the key factors that has made Kickstarter so successful is its focus on creative projects. Unlike other crowdfunding platforms that cater to a wide range of industries, Kickstarter was specifically designed to support artists, musicians, filmmakers, and designers. By creating a space exclusively for these creative individuals, Kickstarter has fostered a strong community that is passionate about supporting innovative and artistic endeavors.

Kickstarter's "all-or-nothing" funding model has also played a significant role in its success. This unique approach requires project creators to set a funding goal and only receive the funds if they reach or exceed that goal within a specified timeframe. This model creates a sense of urgency and encourages backers to support projects they truly believe in. It also provides a level of security for backers, as they know their contributions will only be used if the project has a real chance of success.

Another key aspect that sets Kickstarter apart is its emphasis on rewards-based crowdfunding. Unlike equity crowdfunding, where backers receive a stake in the company or product being funded, Kickstarter focuses on offering exclusive rewards to backers. These rewards can range from a signed copy of a book to a private concert with a musician. This approach allows project creators to offer something unique and valuable to their backers, while also incentivizing them to contribute to the project's success.

Kickstarter's user-friendly platform has also contributed to its popularity. The website is designed to be intuitive and easy to navigate, making it accessible to both project creators and backers. The platform provides a wide range of tools and resources to help project creators showcase their ideas effectively, from project descriptions to high-quality visuals. This attention to detail has helped Kickstarter attract a large and diverse community of users.

One of the most important aspects that sets Kickstarter apart is its commitment to transparency. The platform encourages project creators to provide regular updates on the progress of their projects, keeping backers informed every step of the way. This transparency builds trust between project creators and backers and fosters a sense of community and collaboration. It also helps backers feel more connected to the projects they support, knowing that their contributions are making a tangible difference.

Key Factors That Set Kickstarter Apart

So, what are the key factors that set Kickstarter apart from other crowdfunding websites? In this section, we will explore the unique aspects of Kickstarter that have contributed to its leading position in the crowdfunding industry.

One of the standout features of Kickstarter is its focus on creative projects. Unlike other crowdfunding platforms that cater to a wide range of industries, Kickstarter was specifically designed to support artists, musicians, filmmakers, and designers. By creating a space exclusively for these creative individuals, Kickstarter has fostered a strong community that is passionate about supporting innovative and artistic endeavors. This targeted approach has allowed Kickstarter to cultivate a niche audience that is enthusiastic about contributing to projects they are genuinely interested in.

The "all-or-nothing" funding model is another key factor that sets Kickstarter apart. With this model, project creators must set a funding goal and only receive the funds if they reach or exceed that goal within a specified timeframe. This approach creates a sense of urgency and encourages backers to support projects they truly believe in. It also provides a level of security for backers, as they know their contributions will only be used if the project has a real chance of success. This funding model ensures that project creators have the necessary resources to bring their ideas to life, while also giving backers the confidence that their contributions will have a meaningful impact.

Kickstarter's emphasis on rewards-based crowdfunding is also worth mentioning. Unlike equity crowdfunding, where backers receive a stake in the company or product being funded, Kickstarter focuses on offering exclusive rewards to backers. These rewards can range from a signed copy of a book to a private concert with a musician. This approach allows project creators to offer something unique and valuable to their backers, while also incentivizing them to contribute to the project's success. By providing these exclusive rewards, Kickstarter encourages backers to become invested in the projects they support and helps create a sense of community around each campaign.

The user-friendly platform of Kickstarter has played a significant role in its popularity as well. The website is designed to be intuitive and easy to navigate, making it accessible to both project creators and backers. The platform provides a wide range of tools and resources to help project creators showcase their ideas effectively, from project descriptions to high-quality visuals. This attention to detail has helped Kickstarter attract a large and diverse community of users, ensuring that there is something for everyone on the platform.

Transparency is another key aspect that sets Kickstarter apart. The platform encourages project creators to provide regular updates on the progress of their projects, keeping backers informed every step of the way. This transparency builds trust between project creators and backers, and fosters a sense of community and collaboration. Backers feel more connected to the projects they support, knowing that their contributions are making a tangible difference. Kickstarter has made transparency a priority, and it is evident in the level of engagement and communication between project creators and backers.

In summary, Kickstarter stands out from other crowdfunding platforms for several key factors. Its focus on creative projects, the "all-or-nothing" funding model, rewards-based crowdfunding, user-friendly platform, and commitment to transparency have all contributed to its leading position in the crowdfunding industry. If you are considering crowdfunding for your next project, Kickstarter is a platform that offers the support, resources, and community you need to turn your idea into a reality.

Why Should You Choose Kickstarter for Your Next Project?

When it comes to choosing a crowdfunding platform for your next project, there are many options available. But why should you choose Kickstarter? What makes it stand out from the crowd? In this section, we will explore the key reasons why Kickstarter is the platform of choice for so many creators and entrepreneurs.

First and foremost, Kickstarter has established itself as a leader in the crowdfunding industry. With over a decade of experience, Kickstarter has a proven track record of success. It has facilitated the funding of thousands of projects, ranging from innovative tech gadgets to groundbreaking films. This track record speaks volumes about the credibility and reliability of the platform. By choosing Kickstarter, you can tap into a wealth of expertise and support that can help bring your project to life.

One of the biggest advantages of Kickstarter is its

focused community of backers. Unlike other crowdfunding platforms that cater to a wide range of industries, Kickstarter was specifically designed to support creative projects. This means that the community of backers on Kickstarter is comprised of individuals who are genuinely passionate about art, design, music, and other creative endeavors. By showcasing your project on Kickstarter, you can connect with a target audience that is more likely to resonate with your idea and support it wholeheartedly.

Kickstarter's "all-or-nothing" funding model is another reason why it is a top choice for creators. This model provides a level of security for both project creators and backers. As a creator, you know that you will only receive the funds if you reach or exceed your funding goal. This ensures that you have the necessary resources to bring your project to fruition. As a backer, you can be confident that your contribution will only be used if the project has a real chance of success. This model encourages backers to support projects they truly believe in, knowing that their contributions will have a meaningful impact.

In addition to its funding model, Kickstarter's emphasis on rewards-based crowdfunding is another enticing factor. By offering exclusive rewards to backers, you can create a sense of excitement and exclusivity around your project. These rewards can range from personalized thank you notes to limited-edition merchandise or even once-in-a-lifetime experiences. By providing unique and valuable rewards, you can incentivize backers to contribute to your project and make them feel like they are part of something special.

Another reason to choose Kickstarter is its user-friendly platform. From creating your project page to managing updates and communicating with backers, Kickstarter provides intuitive tools and resources to make the process as smooth as possible. The platform allows you to showcase your project effectively through compelling visuals, detailed descriptions, and engaging videos. With Kickstarter's user-friendly interface, you can focus on what you do best – bringing your creative vision to life.

Lastly, Kickstarter is known for its commitment to transparency and community engagement. Throughout your project's journey, you will have the opportunity to update backers on your progress, share behind-the-scenes insights, and celebrate milestones together. This level of transparency helps build trust and fosters a sense of community.

Backers will feel more connected to your project, knowing that their contributions are making a real difference. Kickstarter's emphasis on community and collaboration sets it apart from other crowdfunding platforms and can greatly enhance your project's success.

Choosing Kickstarter as your crowdfunding platform offers a myriad of benefits. From its proven track record and focused community to its unique funding model and rewards-based approach, Kickstarter provides the support, resources, and community you need to turn your creative vision into a reality. With Kickstarter, you can reach a passionate audience, gain access to valuable expertise, and bring your project to life with the support of backers who truly believe in your idea. So, if you're ready to take the next step in your creative journey, Kickstarter is the platform to choose.

2 Setting the Stage: Pre-Campaign Preparation

So, you have this amazing idea that you're eager to turn into a reality through a Kickstarter campaign. That's fantastic! But before you dive headfirst into launching your campaign, it's crucial to perfect your pitch. The way you present your idea to potential backers can make or break the success of your campaign.

First and foremost, you need to clearly and concisely communicate your idea. Think of your pitch as an elevator pitch – you have a short amount of time to capture someone's attention and convince them that your idea is worth investing in. Start by explaining what problem your product or project solves. What is the pain point that your idea addresses? How will it make people's lives better or easier? You want to make it crystal clear why your idea is valuable and why people should care about it.

In addition to addressing the problem your idea solves, it's also essential to highlight the uniqueness and innovation behind your concept. What sets your idea apart from similar products or projects on the market? Is there a new technology or feature that makes your idea stand out? Showcase what makes your idea special and why it's worth supporting.

Next, think about the emotional connection you can create with your audience. People are more likely to back a project that resonates with them on a personal level. Share your story and the motivation behind your idea. Did a personal experience inspire you? How will your project make a positive impact on society or individuals? Tap into the emotions of your potential backers and make them feel connected to your cause.

Another important aspect to consider when perfecting your pitch is to show rather than tell. People want to see evidence that your idea is viable and will actually work. If you already have a prototype or a demo of your product, make sure to showcase it in your pitch. Seeing is believing, and having something tangible to show can significantly increase the credibility and trustworthiness of your campaign.

Lastly, keep your pitch simple and easy to understand. Avoid using technical jargon or complicated language that might confuse your audience. You want to appeal to a wide range of people, so make sure your pitch is accessible to everyone. Use clear and straightforward language that can be easily grasped by both experts and laypeople.

Understanding Your Market: Research and Validation Strategies for a Successful Campaign

Understanding your market is a critical step in preparing for a successful Kickstarter campaign. Without a thorough understanding of your target audience and their needs, your campaign is likely to fall short. In this section, we will discuss research and validation strategies that will help you gain valuable insights and ensure that your campaign resonates with your audience.

The first step in understanding your market is to identify your target audience. Who are the people most likely to be interested in your product or project? Start by creating a buyer persona, which is a detailed description of your ideal customer. Consider factors such as demographics, interests, and behaviors. By having a clear picture of who your target audience is, you can tailor your campaign to appeal to their specific needs and desires.

Once you have identified your target audience, it's time to conduct market research. Market research involves gathering and analyzing information about your industry, competitors, and potential customers. There are several ways to conduct market research, including surveys, interviews, and focus groups. These methods can provide valuable insights into your audience's preferences, purchasing habits, and pain points. Use this information to refine your campaign messaging and ensure that it resonates with your target audience.

In addition to conducting market research, it's important to validate your idea before launching your campaign. Validation involves testing your product or concept with your target audience to ensure that there is demand for it. One way to validate your idea is to create a minimum viable product (MVP) or a prototype and share it with potential customers for feedback. This allows you to make any necessary improvements before launching your campaign.

Another validation strategy is to run a pre-launch campaign. This involves creating a landing page or a pre-order page where people can express interest in your product or project. By collecting email addresses or pre-orders, you can gauge the level of interest in your idea and determine if there is a market for it. This validation not only provides valuable feedback but also helps build a community of potential backers who are already invested in your idea.

In addition to gathering feedback from your target audience, it's also important to keep an eye on your competitors. Research their campaigns and see what worked well for them and what didn't. Look for any gaps or opportunities in the market that you can capitalize on. By understanding what sets you apart from your competitors, you can highlight your unique value proposition and position yourself effectively in the market.

Understanding your market is an ongoing process. Continuously monitor industry trends, customer feedback, and competitor activities. Stay adaptable and be willing to make changes to your campaign strategy based on new information. By staying in tune with your target audience, you can ensure that your Kickstarter campaign is relevant, impactful, and ultimately successful.

The First Taste of Reality: Importance and Process of Building a Prototype

The first taste of reality in any Kickstarter campaign

comes when you start building a prototype. This is the point where your idea transitions from just a concept to a tangible product that potential backers can see and touch. Building a prototype is a crucial step in the pre-campaign preparation process, as it allows you to test and refine your idea before launching it to the world.

The importance of building a prototype cannot be overstated. It serves as proof of concept, demonstrating that your idea can actually be brought to life. A prototype also gives potential backers a glimpse into what your final product will look like and how it will function. This can help generate excitement and build anticipation for your campaign.

When it comes to building a prototype, there are several factors to consider. The first is deciding what type of prototype to create. There are various levels of prototypes, ranging from a simple mock-up to a fully functional model. The level of complexity will depend on the nature of your idea and the resources available to you.

A simple mock-up can be created using basic materials such as cardboard or foam. This type of prototype allows you to visualize the form and size of your product. It can be useful for testing ergonomics and determining if the design meets your expectations.

If your product involves technology or mechanical components, a functional prototype may be necessary. This type of prototype is closer to the final product and includes working parts and features. It allows you to test the functionality, performance, and user experience of your product.

Building a prototype involves a combination of DIY skills, collaboration, and potentially working with a professional. Depending on your expertise and resources, you may be able to create a prototype on your own. This can be a cost-effective option, especially if you have experience in product development or engineering.

However, if you lack the necessary skills or tools, it may be worth hiring a professional to help you bring your prototype to life. They can provide technical expertise, offer advice on materials and manufacturing processes, and ensure that your prototype accurately represents your vision.

Regardless of the route you choose, it's important to remember that a prototype doesn't have to be perfect. The purpose of building a prototype is to test and iterate on your idea. It's a chance to identify any flaws or areas for improvement before launching your campaign.

Once you have a prototype, it's essential to gather feedback from potential users and incorporate their insights into the development process. Conduct user testing and ask for honest opinions. Pay attention to any pain points or areas of confusion that users encounter. This feedback will help you refine your product and make it more appealing to your target audience.

Setting Realistic Goals for Your Kickstarter Project

Setting realistic goals is a crucial step in preparing for a successful Kickstarter project. It's the stage where your dreams meet the reality of numbers and logistics. Without clear and attainable goals, your campaign may lack direction and fail to attract potential backers. In this section, we'll dive into the process of setting realistic goals for your Kickstarter project and provide some tips to ensure your campaign is set up for success.

First and foremost, it's important to understand the purpose of setting goals for your Kickstarter project. Goals serve as a roadmap, guiding your campaign and providing a clear vision of what you hope to achieve. They give you and your potential backers a tangible target to aim for, creating a sense of purpose and urgency. Setting realistic goals helps manage expectations, both for yourself and your backers, and ensures that your campaign remains focused and achievable.

When setting goals for your Kickstarter project, it's crucial to be specific and measurable. Avoid setting vague goals like "raise as much money as possible" or "get as many backers as we can". Instead, break down your objectives into quantifiable targets. For example, set a funding goal that aligns with the costs of production, marketing, and shipping. Determine the number of backers you want to attract or the level of engagement you want to achieve. By setting specific and measurable goals, you can track your progress and adjust your strategy accordingly.

It's also important to set goals that are attainable and realistic. While it's great to dream big, setting unrealistic goals can set you up for disappointment and potentially damage your reputation. Take into consideration the size of your target audience, the competition in your market, and the level of interest in your product or project. Conduct thorough research and benchmark against similar campaigns to determine what is realistic for your

Kickstarter project. Keep in mind that overpromising and underdelivering can harm your credibility and deter potential backers.

Another factor to consider when setting goals is the duration of your Kickstarter campaign. The length of your campaign can impact the goals you set. A shorter campaign may require more aggressive goals to create a sense of urgency, while a longer campaign may allow for more gradual growth. Take into account the attention span and availability of your target audience, as well as any external factors that may influence their decision to back your project.

Furthermore, consider the rewards and incentives you offer to backers when setting your goals. Ensure that the value of the rewards aligns with the level of funding you hope to achieve. Make sure your rewards are enticing and provide value to your backers. Offering exclusive rewards or limited-edition products can help incentivize potential backers to pledge more and reach your funding goals.

Lastly, don't forget to communicate your goals to your potential backers. Transparency is key when it comes to setting goals. Clearly articulate what you hope to achieve with your Kickstarter project and how their support will contribute to that. Be open about the challenges you may face and how you plan to overcome them. Building trust and demonstrating your commitment to achieving your goals can inspire confidence and encourage backers to support your campaign.

Setting realistic goals for your Kickstarter project is an essential step in the pre-campaign preparation process. It provides focus, direction, and motivation for both you and your potential backers.

Effective Budgeting for A Successful Kickstarter Launch

Financing your Kickstarter campaign is a critical aspect of pre-campaign preparation. Without a well-planned budget, your campaign may not reach its full potential. In this section, we will discuss the importance of effective budgeting and provide some tips to help you navigate the financial aspects of your Kickstarter launch.

First and foremost, it's important to set a realistic funding goal for your campaign. Take into consideration the costs involved in producing and delivering your product or project. Factor in expenses such as manufacturing, packaging, shipping, marketing, and any other operational costs. It's crucial to have a clear understanding of how much money you need to bring your idea to life and ensure that your funding goal aligns with these costs.

In addition to determining your funding goal, it's important to think about how you will allocate the funds you raise. Create a detailed budget that outlines your expenses and revenue projections. Break down your budget into categories such as production, marketing, fulfillment, and miscellaneous expenses. This will help you stay organized and ensure that you have allocated enough funds to each area.

When creating your budget, it's essential to be conservative and account for unexpected costs or delays. It's always better to overestimate your expenses and end up with surplus funds than to underestimate and be caught off guard. Leave room for contingencies and consider setting aside a portion of your funds for unexpected expenses or future development.

In addition to your expenses, it's important to consider the fees associated with running a Kickstarter campaign. Kickstarter charges a 5% fee on the total amount raised, and there may be additional payment processing fees. Factor these fees into your budget to ensure that you are accounting for all costs.

Once you have a clear understanding of your expenses and funding goal, it's time to think about how you will attract backers and generate revenue. Consider your pricing strategy and the rewards you will offer to backers. Take into account the cost of producing and fulfilling these rewards when setting your prices. It's important to strike a balance between offering enticing rewards and ensuring that your campaign remains financially viable.

When setting your reward tiers, think about offering a range of options to cater to different budgets and preferences. Consider offering early bird specials or limited-edition rewards to incentivize backers to pledge more. It's also important to consider any stretch goals you may have. Stretch goals are additional funding milestones that, when reached, unlock new features, upgrades, or products. Make sure to budget for these additional expenses and set realistic stretch goals that align with your funding goal.

Finally, consider your marketing and promotional expenses when budgeting for your Kickstarter campaign. While it's possible to run a successful campaign without spending a significant amount on marketing, it's important to allocate some funds for promotional activities. This can include social media advertising, influencer collaborations, PR efforts, or video production. Determine how much you are willing to invest in marketing and make sure it aligns with your overall budget.

Effective budgeting is crucial for a successful Kickstarter campaign. By setting a realistic funding goal, creating a detailed budget, and accounting for all expenses and revenue sources, you can ensure that your campaign is financially viable and well-prepared for success.

3 Creating a Compelling Campaign Page

One of the most important aspects of a successful Kickstarter campaign is the ability to tell a compelling story. Your story is what will captivate potential backers and make them want to be a part of your project. So how do you craft an irresistible story that will resonate with your audience? Let's dive in and find out.

First and foremost, your story should be authentic and genuine. People connect with stories that are honest and transparent, so don't be afraid to share your personal journey and the challenges you've faced along the way. This will help your backers relate to you on a deeper level and understand why your project is so important to you.

Start by introducing yourself and explaining your background and expertise. Let your audience know why you are the right person to bring this idea to life. Share any relevant experience or qualifications that showcase your ability to execute the project successfully. This will instill confidence in potential backers and make them more likely to support you.

Next, dive into the inspiration behind your project.

What problem are you trying to solve? What gap in the market are you filling? Share the story of how the idea came to be and why it is so important to you. Paint a vivid picture of the problem and explain why it needs to be solved. This will help your backers understand the value of your project and the impact it can have.

Once you've set the stage, it's time to introduce your project and explain how it works. Describe your product or service in detail, highlighting its unique features and benefits. Use visuals, such as images or videos, to help bring your project to life and give potential backers a clear understanding of what they are supporting. Remember, a picture is worth a thousand words, so make sure your visuals are compelling and engaging.

In addition to explaining how your project works, it's important to outline your timeline and goals. Let your backers know what milestones you hope to achieve and how you plan to reach them. This will help create a sense of excitement and urgency, as backers will want to be a part of your journey from start to finish.

Finally, don't forget to include a call to action at the end of your story. Clearly communicate what you need from your backers and how they can get involved. Whether it's making a financial contribution, sharing your campaign on social media, or providing feedback and support, let your audience know how they can help. Make it easy for them to take action and be a part of your success.

Crafting an irresistible story for your Kickstarter campaign takes time and effort, but it is well worth it in the end. By sharing your journey, connecting with your audience, and clearly communicating the value of your project, you can create a story that captivates and inspires. So go ahead, tell your story and bring your passion project to life on Kickstarter. Your audience is waiting to hear from you.

How to Showcase Your Product with Engaging Visuals

When it comes to creating a winning Kickstarter campaign, showcasing your product with engaging visuals is key. Potential backers want to see what they are supporting and get a clear sense of your product's features and benefits. In this section, we'll explore how to effectively showcase your product and captivate your audience with visuals that leave a lasting impression.

First and foremost, high-quality imagery is crucial. Invest in professional product photography or create compelling graphics that accurately represent your product. These visuals should showcase your product from different angles, highlighting its key features and unique selling points. Use images that are visually appealing and capture the essence of what makes your product stand out. Remember, potential backers can't physically touch or try your product, so the visuals you provide need to bridge that gap and create a sense of connection.

In addition to high-quality images, consider incorporating videos into your campaign. Videos are a powerful tool for showcasing your product in action and creating a deeper emotional connection with your audience. A well-produced video can demonstrate how your product works, highlight its benefits, and provide a behind-the-scenes look at the development process. Consider including customer testimonials or endorsements from influencers in your video to add credibility and build trust.

When creating your video, keep it concise and engaging. Attention spans are short, so aim for a length of around two to three minutes. Grab your audience's attention from the start and maintain their interest throughout. Use storytelling techniques, music, and dynamic visuals to create a captivating experience that leaves a lasting impression.

In addition to images and videos, consider creating interactive elements that allow potential backers to experience your product virtually. This could be a 3D model that allows them to rotate and explore your product from different angles, or a virtual demo that lets them interact with a simulation of your product's functionality. These interactive elements can help potential backers visualize the product in a more immersive way and increase their confidence in its quality and value.

Don't forget to include descriptive and engaging captions for your visuals. Use concise and persuasive language to highlight the key features and benefits of your product. Explain how your product solves a problem or improves the lives of your target audience. Keep your captions clear and easy to read, avoiding jargon or overly technical terms. Remember, you want to make it as easy as possible for potential backers to understand and connect with your product.

Finally, consider the layout and design of your campaign page. Use a clean and visually appealing format that allows your visuals to shine. Organize your visuals in a way that guides potential backers through the story of your product, from the initial concept to the final result. Use headings, bullet points, and subheadings to break up the text and make it easy to scan. The overall design of your campaign page should reflect the quality and professionalism of your product.

By showcasing your product with engaging visuals, you can capture the attention and interest of potential backers. Invest in high-quality images, create compelling videos, and consider interactive elements that allow your audience to experience your product virtually. Craft descriptive and engaging captions to highlight the key features and benefits of your product. Finally, pay attention to the layout and design of your campaign page to create a visually appealing and cohesive presentation. With these strategies, you'll be well on your way to creating a compelling Kickstarter campaign that leaves a lasting impression on potential backers.

Setting Up Reward Tiers that Resonate with your Audience

The right rewards can entice potential backers to pledge their support and help you reach your funding goal. In this section, we'll explore how to create reward tiers that not only attract backers but also provide value and incentives that resonate with your audience.

1. Understand your audience: Before you start brainstorming reward ideas, it's essential to have a clear understanding of your target audience. Who are they? What are their interests, desires, and motivations? What are they willing to invest in? By knowing your audience inside out, you can tailor your reward tiers to meet their needs and preferences.

2. Offer a range of rewards: When it comes to reward tiers, variety is key. Offer a range of rewards at different price points to accommodate various budgets. Some backers may be looking for a small token of appreciation, while others may be willing to make a significant contribution for an exclusive experience. By providing options, you cater to a wider audience and increase the likelihood of attracting more backers.

3. Make it exclusive: Exclusive rewards create a sense of urgency and FOMO (fear of missing out) among potential backers. Offer limited edition products, early access to your project, or one-of-a-kind experiences that are only available through your Kickstarter campaign. This exclusivity adds value to your rewards and makes backers feel like

they're part of something special.

4. Provide social proof: Backers want to know that they're supporting a project with a reputable and credible creator. Incorporate social proof into your reward tiers by offering endorsements or testimonials from influencers or industry experts. This not only boosts your credibility but also increases the perceived value of your rewards.

5. Bundle rewards strategically: Bundle rewards allow you to offer more value to backers while maximizing your funding potential. Combine different rewards into tiers that make sense and provide a comprehensive package. For example, if you're launching a new book, consider bundling it with a signed copy, a limited edition bookmark, and a behind-the-scenes video. By bundling rewards, you can increase the perceived value and appeal to backers who want more for their pledge.

6. Create early bird rewards: Early bird rewards are a fantastic way to create a sense of excitement and incentivize backers to pledge early. Offer exclusive discounts or additional perks to the first backers who support your campaign. This strategy not only helps you gain early momentum but also encourages backers to share your campaign with their network to secure the limited early bird

rewards.

7. Communicate the impact: When creating reward tiers, clearly communicate the impact that backers will have by supporting your project. Show them how their contribution will make a difference and what the project's ultimate goals are. Backers are more likely to pledge when they can see the positive impact their support will have.

8. Keep fulfillment in mind: Finally, when designing your reward tiers, make sure to consider the logistics and cost of fulfilling each reward. Ensure that you can deliver on your promises within a reasonable timeframe and budget. Nothing is more disappointing for backers than a campaign that fails to fulfill its rewards, so plan accordingly and be transparent about any potential challenges.

By setting up reward tiers that resonate with your audience, you can attract more backers and increase your chances of reaching your funding goal. Understand your audience, offer a range of rewards, make them exclusive, provide social proof, strategically bundle rewards, create early bird incentives, communicate the impact, and keep fulfillment in mind. With these strategies in place, your Kickstarter campaign will have a much higher chance of success.

Writing a Captivating Pitch for your Kickstarter Campaign

The pitch is the heart and soul of your Kickstarter campaign. It's the part that will capture the attention of potential backers and convince them to support your project. So how do you write a captivating pitch that leaves a lasting impression? Let's dive in and find out.

First and foremost, it's important to grab your audience's attention right from the start. Your opening line should be compelling and make them want to continue reading. Whether it's a thought-provoking question, a bold statement, or a captivating story, find a way to immediately hook your audience and make them curious about your project.

Next, clearly communicate what your project is all about. Explain the problem you're solving, the product or service you're offering, and why it's unique and valuable. Keep it concise and to the point, but also make sure to convey your passion and enthusiasm for your project. Show your audience why you believe in it and why they should too.

When writing your pitch, it's important to consider your audience. Put yourself in their shoes and think about what would resonate with them. What are their needs, desires, and motivations? How does your project align with those? Tailor your pitch to address their concerns and highlight the benefits they will receive by supporting your project.

To make your pitch more persuasive, consider incorporating social proof. Show potential backers that others have already believed in your project and have had positive experiences with it. Include testimonials from previous supporters or endorsements from influencers in your field. This not only adds credibility to your campaign but also instills confidence in potential backers.

In addition to social proof, it's important to communicate a sense of urgency in your pitch. Let your audience know why they should support your project now and not later. Are there limited edition rewards? Is there a specific timeline or deadline they need to be aware of? Creating a sense of urgency will help encourage potential backers to take action and pledge their support sooner rather than later.

When crafting your pitch, it's important to be transparent and honest about the risks and challenges involved in your project. Potential backers appreciate transparency and want to know that you've considered the potential roadblocks. Clearly communicate any potential obstacles and explain how you plan to overcome them. This will show your audience that you've thought through the project thoroughly and are prepared to handle any challenges that may arise.

Lastly, don't forget to include a clear call to action in your pitch. Let potential backers know what you need from them and how they can get involved. Clearly communicate the reward tiers you've set up and explain the value they will receive by supporting your project. Make it easy for them to take action and provide a simple way for them to contribute.

Writing a captivating pitch for your Kickstarter campaign is a crucial step in reaching your funding goal. By grabbing your audience's attention, clearly communicating the value of your project, incorporating social proof and urgency, and including a clear call to action, you can create a pitch that captivates and inspires potential backers.

Crafting a compelling Kickstarter campaign is no easy feat. It takes time, effort, and careful planning. By following the steps outlined in this guide, you can increase your chances of creating a winning Kickstarter campaign. From crafting an irresistible story and showcasing your product with engaging visuals to setting up reward tiers that resonate with your audience and writing a captivating pitch, every aspect of your campaign plays a crucial role in its success. So take the time to carefully craft each section of your campaign and don't be afraid to ask for feedback along the way. With the right approach, you can create a Kickstarter campaign that stands out, attracts backers, and brings your passion project to life.

4 Building Your Tribe: Pre-Launch Marketing

Launching a Kickstarter campaign is an exciting journey, but it's crucial to generate buzz and anticipation among potential backers before the big launch. A well-crafted teaser campaign can be the key to capturing people's attention and getting them excited about your project. In this section, we will explore some strategies and tips to help you create the perfect teaser campaign for your Kickstarter.

Firstly, it's important to understand the purpose of a teaser campaign. The goal is to give potential backers a taste of what your project is all about and build intrigue and excitement. You want to pique their curiosity and leave them wanting more. So, how do you go about crafting an effective teaser campaign? Let's dive in.

1. Teaser Video: Create a compelling and visually appealing teaser video that introduces your project in a concise and engaging manner. Keep it short and snappy, focusing on the most exciting aspects of your project. Use visuals, animations, or graphics that represent your project and captivate your audience. A teaser video can be an excellent tool

to build anticipation and generate excitement among potential backers.

2. Sneak Peeks: Offer sneak peeks of your project to tease your audience. It could be a glimpse of a new feature, a behind-the-scenes photo, or a short excerpt from your upcoming book or album. These sneak peeks give your audience a taste of what's to come and make them eager for more.

3. Countdown: Create a countdown timer on your website or social media platforms to generate a sense of urgency and build excitement leading up to the launch of your Kickstarter campaign. People love anticipation, and a countdown creates a buzz and motivates potential backers to be ready when the campaign goes live.

4. Mystery and Intrigue: Incorporate an element of mystery and intrigue into your teaser campaign. Leave some questions unanswered, hint at surprises, or offer cryptic clues about your project. This sense of mystery will keep potential backers engaged and curious to learn more.

5. Engage your Audience: Use your teaser campaign as an opportunity to start building a community around your project. Encourage potential backers to sign up for email updates or

join a pre-launch mailing list. This not only allows you to keep them informed about your project but also enables you to gauge interest and gather valuable feedback.

6. Collaborate with Influencers: Consider collaborating with influencers or relevant industry experts who align with your project. Reach out to them and offer exclusive access or sneak peeks in exchange for their support and promotion. This can significantly amplify your reach and bring in a new audience of potential backers.

Remember, the key to a successful teaser campaign is to generate curiosity, excitement, and a sense of anticipation. Make your audience feel like they are part of something special and unique. By crafting a compelling teaser campaign, you lay the foundation for a successful Kickstarter launch and build a strong and supportive community around your project.

How to Leverage Social Media for Your Pre-Launch Marketing

Social media has become a powerful tool for connecting with audiences, spreading the word about your projects, and building a loyal community of supporters. When it comes to pre-launch marketing for your Kickstarter campaign, leveraging social media can be a game-changer. It allows you to reach a wide audience, generate excitement, and engage with potential backers on a personal level. In this section, we will explore some tips and strategies to help you leverage social media effectively for your pre-launch marketing.

1. Choose the Right Platforms: With so many social media platforms available, it's important to focus your efforts on the ones that are most relevant to your target audience. Research which platforms your potential backers frequent the most and invest your time and resources in those channels. Whether it's Facebook, Instagram, Twitter, or YouTube, understanding your audience's preferences will help you tailor your content and engage with them effectively.

2. Create Engaging Content: Social media users are bombarded with content every day, so it's crucial to create content that stands out and captures their attention. Use compelling visuals, videos, and graphics to make your posts eye-catching and shareable. Incorporate storytelling elements to create an emotional connection with your audience. Ask questions, run polls, or create interactive content to encourage engagement and foster a sense of community.

3. Consistency is Key: Building a social media presence takes time and consistency. Create a content calendar and schedule regular posts to keep your audience engaged. Aim for a mix of content, including updates about your project, behind-the-scenes glimpses, relevant industry news, and interactive posts. Consistency not only keeps your project at the forefront of your audience's minds but also demonstrates your dedication and professionalism.

4. Engage with Your Audience: Social media is a two-way street. It's not just about broadcasting your message; it's also about building relationships with your audience. Respond to comments, messages, and mentions promptly and authentically. Show genuine interest in your audience's opinions and feedback. By actively engaging with your audience, you make them feel valued and invested in your project.

5. Collaborate with Influencers: Influencers have become an integral part of social media marketing. They have dedicated followers who trust their opinions and recommendations. Identify influencers who align with your project and reach out to them for collaboration opportunities. This could involve hosting a live Q&A session, doing a

product review, or offering exclusive discounts to their followers. Influencers can help you expand your reach and tap into new audiences.

6. Utilize Hashtags: Hashtags are a powerful way to increase the visibility of your social media posts. Research popular and relevant hashtags in your niche and incorporate them into your content. Additionally, consider creating a unique hashtag for your project to encourage your audience to join the conversation and share their excitement.

7. Run Contests and Giveaways: Contests and giveaways are excellent tactics to generate buzz and increase engagement on social media. Create a contest that encourages your audience to share, tag friends, or create user-generated content related to your project. Offer exciting rewards or exclusive access to your project as prizes. Contests and giveaways not only generate excitement but also help you reach new potential backers through the social networks of your existing audience.

Leveraging social media for your pre-launch marketing can significantly boost your Kickstarter campaign's visibility, engagement, and chances of success. Remember, the key is to provide valuable and engaging content, be consistent in your efforts, and actively engage with your audience. Social media offers an incredible platform for building anticipation and excitement around your project, so make the most of it!

Tips and Tricks to Build a Robust Email List

Building a robust email list is a crucial step in your pre-launch marketing strategy for your Kickstarter campaign. By gathering a list of interested individuals who have opted to receive updates from you, you can directly reach out to them with exciting news and updates about your project. In this section, we will explore some tips and tricks to help you build a strong and engaged email list.

1. Create an Eye-Catching Landing Page: Your landing page is where potential backers will provide their email addresses to join your mailing list. Make sure your landing page is visually appealing, concise, and clearly communicates the value they will receive by joining your list. Use attention-grabbing headlines, compelling visuals, and a strong call-to-action to encourage visitors to sign up.

2. Offer Exclusive Content or Incentives: In order to entice potential backers to join your email list, consider offering exclusive content or incentives. This could be a free downloadable guide, a sneak

peek of your project, or access to behind-the-scenes updates. By providing something of value, you give people a reason to willingly share their email addresses with you.

3. Run Contests and Giveaways: Running contests and giveaways can be an effective way to build your email list. Create a contest that encourages participants to sign up for your email updates or share your project with their friends in exchange for a chance to win a prize. This not only incentivizes people to join your list but also helps you increase your reach through their networks.

4. Optimize your Sign-Up Form: Make sure your email sign-up form is user-friendly and easy to fill out. Keep it simple by asking for only the necessary information, such as their name and email address. Consider using a two-step opt-in process, where users click a button or checkbox to indicate their interest before filling out the form. This can help increase conversions and reduce friction.

5. Use Pop-Ups and Exit Intent Overlays: Pop-ups and exit intent overlays can be effective tools for capturing email addresses. By displaying a pop-up when a user enters or exits your website, you can offer them the opportunity to join your email list. Make sure your pop-up is visually appealing,

concise, and provides a clear value proposition to entice visitors to sign up.

6. Promote your Email List on Social Media: Leverage your social media platforms to promote your email list and encourage followers to sign up. Create compelling graphics, videos, or posts that highlight the benefits of joining your email list and include a clear call-to-action with a link to your landing page. Additionally, consider using social media advertising to target potential backers and drive them to your landing page.

7. Guest Blogging and Collaborations: Seek opportunities to guest blog or collaborate with others in your industry or niche. By providing valuable content or offering to be a guest on relevant podcasts or webinars, you can reach a new audience and direct them to your landing page to join your email list. Make sure to include a call-to-action or link to your landing page in your guest posts or collaborations.

8. Utilize Email Segmentation: As your email list grows, consider segmenting your subscribers based on their interests or level of engagement. This allows you to tailor your email content and offers to specific segments, increasing the likelihood of conversion. By providing personalized

and relevant content, you can build a stronger connection with your subscribers and increase their likelihood of backing your project.

Building a robust email list takes time and effort, but it is a valuable asset for your Kickstarter campaign. By implementing these tips and tricks, you can attract interested individuals, engage with them through regular updates, and increase the chances of converting them into backers. Remember to provide value, be consistent with your communication, and always respect your subscribers' privacy and preferences.

Why Engaging Influencers and Early Supporters is Key

When it comes to launching a successful Kickstarter campaign, engaging influencers and early supporters can be a game-changer. These individuals have the power to amplify your reach, increase your visibility, and generate a buzz around your project. In this section, we will discuss why engaging influencers and early supporters is key to the success of your Kickstarter campaign.

1. Expanding Your Reach: Influencers have built a dedicated following of individuals who trust their opinions and recommendations. By collaborating

with influencers who align with your project, you can tap into their audience and reach a whole new group of potential backers. Their endorsement and promotion of your campaign can significantly expand your reach and attract more attention to your project.

2. Leveraging Credibility: Influencers are seen as experts or authorities in their respective fields. When they support your project, their endorsement adds credibility and legitimacy to your campaign. Potential backers are more likely to trust the recommendation of an influencer they follow and admire. By engaging influencers, you can leverage their credibility to build trust and encourage more individuals to back your project.

3. Accessing Targeted Audiences: Influencers have cultivated a specific niche audience that aligns with their interests or expertise. By collaborating with influencers who have a similar target audience as your project, you can access a group of individuals who are more likely to be interested in what you have to offer. These targeted audiences have a higher likelihood of converting into backers, making them valuable for the success of your Kickstarter campaign.

4. Generating Social Proof: Early supporters, such

as friends, family, and loyal followers, play a crucial role in generating social proof for your Kickstarter campaign. When these individuals back your project early on, it creates a sense of credibility and trust for potential backers who are considering supporting your campaign. People are more likely to back a project that has already gained some traction and support. By engaging early supporters, you can leverage their backing to generate social proof and attract more backers.

5. Building a Strong Community: Engaging influencers and early supporters is not just about gaining their support, but also about building a strong and supportive community around your project. These individuals become advocates for your campaign, sharing it with their networks, and encouraging others to back your project. By fostering a sense of community and collaboration, you create a dedicated group of backers who are invested in your success.

6. Increased Visibility and Promotion: When influencers and early supporters back your project, they often promote it on their social media platforms, websites, or blogs. This exposure can significantly increase the visibility of your campaign and attract more attention. Their promotion can take various forms, such as featuring your project

in a blog post, creating content about it on YouTube or Instagram, or even hosting a live event or webinar to discuss your project. By engaging influencers and early supporters, you open up avenues for increased visibility and promotion of your Kickstarter campaign.

Engaging influencers and early supporters can be a powerful strategy to generate interest and excitement for your Kickstarter campaign. They have the ability to expand your reach, increase your visibility, build credibility, and generate social proof. By leveraging their support, you can attract a targeted audience, build a strong community, and increase the chances of reaching your funding goal. So don't underestimate the power of influencers and early supporters – they could be the key to the success of your Kickstarter campaign.

5 Launch Day Strategies

The day has finally arrived. Months of preparation, planning, and anticipation culminate in this one crucial moment: the launch of your Kickstarter campaign. It's an exciting time, but also a nerve-wracking one. Will your project capture the attention of backers? Will you be able to generate enough momentum to propel your campaign to success? The answer lies in the importance of building momentum for launch day.

Launching your Kickstarter campaign with momentum is crucial for several reasons. First and foremost, it sets the tone for the entire duration of your campaign. A strong start creates a sense of excitement and urgency among potential backers, making them more likely to support your project early on. When people see that others are already backing your campaign, it creates a snowball effect, encouraging more people to join in and contribute.

Building momentum for launch day also helps establish credibility and trust. When potential backers see that your campaign is off to a strong start, they are more likely to view you as a legitimate and trustworthy project creator. It demonstrates that you have put in the time and effort to plan a successful campaign and that others believe in your project enough to support it.

Additionally, building momentum early on can attract the attention of the Kickstarter community and increase your campaign's visibility. Kickstarter features projects that are trending and gaining momentum on its website, which can lead to additional exposure and a wider audience. The more eyes on your campaign, the greater the chances of reaching your funding goal.

So, how do you go about building momentum for launch day? One key strategy is to create a buzz around your project in the weeks leading up to the launch. Start by reaching out to your existing network, such as friends, family, and colleagues, and share the news about your upcoming campaign. Encourage them to spread the word and get others excited about your project.

Another effective way to build momentum is to offer exclusive incentives or early bird rewards to early backers. These can be limited in quantity or time, creating a sense of urgency and motivating people to support your project right from the start. By offering something unique and valuable, you can generate buzz and attract backers who want to be part of the excitement.

In addition to these strategies, utilizing social media platforms can be instrumental in building momentum. Create engaging content that showcases your project and its potential impact. Use visually appealing images and videos to grab people's attention and share updates and progress leading up to launch day. Encourage your followers to like, comment, and share your posts, helping to spread the word organically.

Finally, consider collaborating with influencers or relevant media outlets to further amplify your campaign. Reach out to bloggers, journalists, or podcasters who cover topics related to your project and offer them an exclusive sneak peek or interview opportunity. Getting your project featured in the media can significantly boost your visibility and attract a wider audience of potential backers.

Building momentum for launch day is not something that happens by chance. It requires careful planning, strategic outreach, and engaging content creation. By implementing these strategies, you can give your Kickstarter campaign the best possible chance of achieving its goals and making your project a reality.

In the next section, we will delve into the role of campaign updates and how they can contribute to the success of your Kickstarter campaign.

Campaign Updates and Their Role in Success

Campaign updates play a vital role in keeping your backers informed, engaged, and excited about your project. They are an effective tool for maintaining momentum and building a supportive community around your campaign.

Regular updates serve multiple purposes. Firstly, they allow you to share progress and milestones with your backers. This not only keeps them informed about the development of your project but also shows them that you are actively working towards bringing your vision to life. It demonstrates your commitment and dedication to delivering on your promises.

In addition to keeping your backers informed, updates also provide an opportunity to generate buzz and excitement. By sharing behind-the-scenes insights, sneak peeks, and exclusive content, you can give your backers a sense of being part of something special. This fosters a feeling of ownership and connection, making them more likely to continue supporting your campaign and spreading the word to others.

When crafting your updates, it's important to strike

a balance between being informative and engaging. Use visual content such as photos, videos, or infographics to make your updates visually appealing and captivating. Share stories or anecdotes that highlight the impact and value of your project. This personal touch creates an emotional connection with your backers and enhances their sense of investment in your campaign.

Timing is also crucial when it comes to updates. Regular and consistent communication is key, but be mindful not to overwhelm your backers with too many updates in a short period. This can lead to information overload and fatigue. Instead, aim for a steady stream of updates, spaced out strategically throughout the duration of your campaign. This keeps your backers engaged without overwhelming them.

Another important aspect of updates is actively involving your backers in the process. Encourage them to share their thoughts, suggestions, or ideas in the comments section of your updates. This fosters a sense of community and collaboration, making your backers feel like valued participants in your project rather than just passive observers. Responding to their comments and engaging in conversations also demonstrates your commitment to building a supportive community.

To make your updates even more impactful, consider incorporating milestones or stretch goals. These are additional targets or achievements that you set for your campaign beyond the initial funding goal. Milestones and stretch goals can be tied to specific funding amounts or backer numbers and provide incentives for your backers to spread the word and recruit others to join in supporting your campaign. Sharing updates that highlight progress towards these goals can help generate excitement and motivate your backers to continue supporting your campaign.

Lastly, don't forget to express gratitude in your updates. Take the time to thank your backers for their support and acknowledge their contributions. This shows your appreciation and reinforces the sense of community and partnership you are building. Gratitude goes a long way in creating a positive and supportive atmosphere around your campaign.

Engaging Your Backers: Creating a Supportive Community

Engaging your backers is a crucial part of this process, as it fosters a sense of connection, builds trust, and encourages ongoing support. In this section, we will discuss some strategies for creating a supportive community of backers and keeping them engaged throughout your campaign.

1. Personalize Your Communications:

One of the most effective ways to engage your backers is to make your communications personal. Address them by name, thank them for their support, and express genuine appreciation for their contributions. This personal touch goes a long way in making your backers feel valued and acknowledged. Whether it's through campaign updates, emails, or social media interactions, take the time to connect with your backers on an individual level.

2. Be Responsive and Accessible:

Engaging your backers requires being responsive and accessible. Respond promptly to comments, messages, and inquiries. Take the time to address their concerns, answer their questions, and provide updates when needed. By being transparent and open to communication, you demonstrate your commitment to building a supportive community. This responsiveness not only keeps your backers engaged but also helps to build trust and credibility.

3. Foster a Sense of Community:

Creating a supportive community involves more than just one-way communication. Encourage your backers to interact with each other by facilitating conversations and fostering a sense of community. This can be done through comments sections, forums, or dedicated social media groups. Encourage backers to share their experiences, offer feedback, and even collaborate with each other. By facilitating these interactions, you not only deepen the sense of community but also empower your backers to become advocates for your project.

4. Offer Exclusive Backer Benefits:

Reward your backers with exclusive benefits and incentives to further engage them and make them feel special. This can include early access to project updates, limited-edition rewards, or even involvement in decision-making processes. By offering these exclusive benefits, you not only show your appreciation for their support but also create a sense of exclusivity and exclusivity that can motivate them to continue supporting your campaign.

5. Show Progress and Impact:

Keeping your backers engaged involves

consistently showcasing the progress and impact of your project. Regularly share updates, photos, and videos that highlight the milestones you have achieved and the difference your project is making. This visual storytelling not only keeps your backers informed but also creates an emotional connection by showing them the tangible results of their support. By regularly sharing progress and impact, you build excitement and inspire continued support.

6. Involve Backers in Decision-Making:

Make your backers feel like active participants in your project by involving them in decision-making processes. Seek their input, opinions, and feedback on key aspects of your project. This can include everything from design choices to stretch goals and future plans. By involving your backers in these decisions, you show them that their opinions matter and that their support is instrumental in shaping the project's success.

7. Express Gratitude:

Never underestimate the power of gratitude. Express your appreciation to your backers regularly and sincerely. Thank them for their support, share stories of how their contributions are making a difference, and celebrate the milestones you achieve together. Expressing gratitude not only strengthens the bond between you and your backers but also creates a positive and supportive atmosphere within your community.

Engaging your backers and creating a supportive community is not a one-time effort; it requires consistent communication, responsiveness, and a genuine commitment to building relationships. By implementing these strategies, you can create a community of backers who are not just supporting your project but also advocating for its success. When you have a strong and engaged community behind you, the chances of reaching your funding goal and turning your project into a reality are significantly increased.

Leverage Press and Media Coverage: Spreading the Word Effectively

Leveraging press and media coverage is a crucial aspect of maximizing the reach and impact of your Kickstarter campaign. By spreading the word effectively, you can attract a wider audience, generate buzz, and increase your chances of reaching your funding goal. In this section, we will explore some strategies to help you effectively leverage press and media coverage for your campaign.

1. Research and Target Relevant Outlets:

Before reaching out to the press, take the time to research and identify media outlets that are relevant to your project. Look for publications, blogs, podcasts, or influencers that cover topics related to your campaign. This will ensure that you are targeting an audience that is already interested in your niche or industry, increasing the chances of capturing their attention and support.

2. Craft a Compelling Press Release:

A well-crafted press release is essential for effectively communicating your campaign to the media. Make sure to include all the necessary information about your project, such as its unique selling points, the problem it solves, and any notable milestones or achievements. Use a concise and engaging writing style to capture the interest of journalists and make them want to learn more.

3. Personalize Your Outreach:

When reaching out to journalists or influencers, personalize your emails or messages to make them feel more personal and tailored to their specific interests. Mention why you believe their audience would be interested in your campaign and highlight any unique angles or stories that make your project stand out. This personalized approach increases the chances of getting a positive response and coverage.

4. Offer Exclusive Sneak Peeks or Interviews:

To entice journalists or influencers to cover your campaign, offer them exclusive access to behind-the-scenes content, sneak peeks, or interview opportunities. This can create a sense of exclusivity and urgency, making them more likely to feature your project. Exclusive content also provides value to their audience, giving them a reason to engage with your campaign and potentially become backers themselves.

5. Build Relationships with Journalists and Influencers:

Building relationships with journalists and influencers in your niche can be incredibly valuable for the long-term success of your campaign and future projects. Engage with their content, share their articles or posts, and offer insights or comments on topics they cover. By establishing yourself as an active and supportive member of their community, you increase the chances of them taking an interest in your campaign and providing coverage.

6. Utilize Social Media to Amplify Coverage:

Once you start receiving press coverage, make sure to amplify it on your social media platforms. Share the articles, interviews, or features and tag the journalists or influencers who covered your campaign. This not only helps you reach a wider audience but also strengthens the relationship with the media outlets and encourages them to continue supporting your project.

7. Be Responsive and Grateful:

When journalists or influencers do cover your campaign, make sure to respond promptly and express gratitude for their support. Thank them publicly on social media, share their coverage with your backers, and consider offering them exclusive updates or additional content in the future. By being responsive and grateful, you foster positive relationships and increase the chances of future coverage.

In summary, leveraging press and media coverage is a powerful way to spread the word about your Kickstarter campaign and attract a wider audience of potential backers. By researching and targeting relevant outlets, crafting compelling press releases, personalizing your outreach, offering exclusives, building relationships, amplifying coverage on social media, and being responsive and grateful, you can effectively leverage the power of the media to maximize the success of your campaign. Remember, a well-executed media strategy can significantly increase your visibility and help you reach your funding goals, so don't underestimate its importance in your launch day tactics.

6 Mid-Campaign: Maintaining Momentum

The mid-campaign slump. It's a phrase that strikes fear into the hearts of Kickstarter creators everywhere. After the initial rush of backers and funding, it's not uncommon for momentum to slow down. The excitement that once filled the air can quickly dissipate, leaving creators feeling disheartened and unsure of how to keep the energy alive.

But here's the thing: the mid-campaign stall doesn't have to be the end of the road. In fact, it can be a valuable opportunity to power through and come out stronger on the other side. So, how exactly do you overcome the dreaded mid-campaign stall? Let's dive in and find out.

First and foremost, it's important to remember that launching a Kickstarter campaign is a marathon, not a sprint. It's natural for things to slow down a bit in the middle. Instead of letting this stall discourage you, use it as a chance to evaluate your progress and make adjustments as needed. Take a step back and assess what's working and what isn't. Are there any patterns or trends in the data? Use this information to refine your approach and push forward.

One effective strategy for maintaining momentum during the mid-campaign phase is introducing stretch goals. Stretch goals are additional milestones or features that can be unlocked as the campaign reaches certain funding levels. They give backers something to look forward to and can reignite excitement for your project. Consider what additional value you can offer to backers and create stretch goals that align with your project's vision. This not only helps maintain interest but also encourages backers to increase their pledges in order to unlock these exciting new additions.

Transparency is another key factor in overcoming the mid-campaign slump. Be open and honest with your backers about any challenges or setbacks you may be facing. They are your biggest supporters and will appreciate your honesty. Whether it's a delay in production or unexpected hurdles, sharing these details shows that you are committed to delivering a high-quality project. This level of transparency can build trust and strengthen the bond between you and your backers, ultimately leading to increased support and enthusiasm.

In addition to transparency, take the time to actively

engage with your backers. Respond to comments, answer questions, and provide updates regularly. By staying active and engaged, you show your backers that their support is valued and that you are committed to delivering on your promises. This not only helps maintain momentum but can also attract new backers who are impressed by your dedication and responsiveness.

Lastly, harness the power of backer data to drive change. Analyze the data from your campaign to gain insights into your backers' preferences, demographics, and behaviors. Are there any trends that stand out? Use this information to make adjustments to your campaign strategy. For example, if you notice a specific demographic showing strong interest in your project, consider targeting your marketing efforts towards that group. By leveraging backer data, you can make informed decisions that will help propel your campaign forward.

The mid-campaign slump may seem daunting, but it doesn't have to be the end of the road. By introducing stretch goals, addressing challenges transparently, and analyzing backer data for adjustments, you can maintain momentum and keep the energy alive. Remember, the key is to stay motivated and determined. Power through the stall, and the success of your Kickstarter campaign will be within reach.

Igniting Excitement with Stretch Goals

As the mid-campaign slump sets in, it's crucial to find ways to reignite the excitement and keep the momentum going. One powerful strategy for doing this is by introducing stretch goals. Stretch goals are additional milestones or features that can be unlocked as the campaign reaches certain funding levels. They provide backers with something to look forward to and can bring a renewed sense of excitement to your project.

So, how do you go about creating effective stretch goals? The first step is to assess what additional value you can offer to backers. Consider what would enhance your project and align with its overall vision. This could be anything from additional content, upgraded materials, or even exclusive merchandise. The key is to offer something that your backers will find enticing and that adds value to their support.

Once you've determined what your stretch goals will be, it's important to set funding thresholds for unlocking them. These thresholds should be realistic and attainable based on your current funding levels. You want to strike a balance between offering exciting stretch goals and not setting the bar too high, as this can lead to disappointment if they are not reached.

When introducing stretch goals, it's essential to communicate them effectively to your backers. Update your campaign page, send out backer updates, and share the news on your social media platforms. Be sure to clearly explain what each stretch goal entails and how it will enhance the project. Use visual aids such as graphics or images to make the goals more enticing and easier to understand. This will help create a sense of anticipation and motivate backers to increase their pledges to unlock these exciting new additions.

Stretch goals can also be an opportunity to foster community engagement and interaction. Encourage your backers to share their ideas and suggestions for additional stretch goals. This not only gives them a sense of ownership and involvement in the project but also helps generate excitement and interest among the backer community. By actively involving your backers in the stretch goal process, you not only increase the chances of reaching funding milestones but also strengthen the overall bond between you and your backers.

To keep the momentum going, it's important to periodically update your backers on the progress of the campaign and the status of the stretch goals. Share the achievements reached so far and highlight the next stretch goal that is within reach. This creates a sense of accomplishment and motivates backers to continue supporting the campaign. It also serves as a reminder that their pledges are making a difference and driving the project forward.

Remember, stretch goals are not just about unlocking additional features or rewards; they are also about creating a sense of excitement and anticipation among your backers. By introducing stretch goals, you give your backers something to look forward to and a reason to continue supporting your campaign. It shows them that you are committed to delivering an exceptional project and that their support is valued.

Tackling Campaign Hurdles with Transparency

Launching a Kickstarter campaign is an exhilarating experience. The early days are filled with excitement as backers flock to support your project and funding begins to roll in. But what happens when the initial rush fades and the mid-campaign slump sets in? This is where many creators face their biggest challenge. However, it's important not to lose heart. Instead, tackle these campaign hurdles with transparency to maintain momentum and keep the energy alive.

Transparency is key when it comes to addressing campaign hurdles. It's natural for setbacks or challenges to arise during the course of your Kickstarter campaign. Whether it's a delay in production, unexpected expenses, or other obstacles, it's crucial to communicate these issues with your backers openly and honestly. Sharing this information shows that you value their support and are committed to delivering on your promises.

When addressing challenges transparently, it's important to provide regular updates to your backers. Keep them informed of any changes, setbacks, or adjustments to the project timeline. This not only keeps them in the loop but also demonstrates your dedication to keeping them informed and involved. By being transparent about the challenges you face, you build trust and strengthen the relationship with your backers.

In addition to providing updates, it's also helpful to share the steps you are taking to overcome these challenges. Outline the actions you are implementing to address the issue at hand.

Whether it's finding alternative suppliers, adjusting production timelines, or seeking additional funding, sharing your strategies and progress shows that you are actively working towards resolving the hurdle. This level of transparency reassures backers that you are committed to finding solutions and delivering on your promises.

When addressing campaign hurdles transparently, it's important to remain positive and focused on finding solutions. Be transparent about the challenges, but also convey your determination and optimism in overcoming them. Share your passion for the project and your unwavering commitment to delivering a high-quality final product. This positivity can be contagious and will help maintain the enthusiasm of your backers.

In addition to being transparent about challenges, it's important to encourage open communication with your backers. Create channels for them to ask questions, provide feedback, and share their concerns. Respond promptly and personally to each inquiry, demonstrating that you value their input and are committed to addressing any issues that may arise. This level of engagement not only helps to resolve any concerns but also builds a strong community around your project.

Furthermore, use your transparent communication as an opportunity to ask for support and collaboration from your backers. Let them know that their input is valued and that their suggestions and ideas are taken into consideration. This creates a sense of ownership among backers and makes them feel more invested in the success of your project. By involving them in the problem-solving process, you can harness their support and creativity to overcome any hurdles.

Transparency is not only important during the mid-campaign slump but throughout the entire Kickstarter campaign. By being open and honest about your challenges, setbacks, and progress, you build trust with your backers and maintain their support and enthusiasm. Keep them informed through regular updates, share the steps you are taking to overcome hurdles, and encourage open communication. By tackling campaign hurdles with transparency, you can overcome obstacles and keep the momentum going, ensuring the success of your Kickstarter campaign.

Harnessing Backer Data to Drive Change

Harnessing backer data is a powerful tool that can

drive change and help you overcome the mid-campaign slump. By analyzing the data from your Kickstarter campaign, you can gain valuable insights into your backers' preferences, demographics, and behaviors. This information can then be used to make informed decisions and adjustments to your campaign strategy, ultimately propelling your project forward.

One of the first things to analyze in your backer data is the demographics of your backers. Are there any trends or patterns that stand out? For example, you may notice that a specific age group or geographic location is showing strong interest in your project. This information can be used to tailor your marketing efforts and target those demographics more effectively. By reaching the right audience, you increase your chances of attracting new backers and maintaining momentum.

In addition to demographics, it's important to analyze your backers' preferences and behaviors. Are there any common characteristics or interests among your backers? This information can help you identify potential partnerships or collaborations that align with your project. For example, if you notice that a significant portion of your backers are interested in sustainable products, you may consider teaming up with eco-friendly brands or organizations. By leveraging your backer data, you can make strategic decisions that resonate with your audience and keep them engaged.

Backer data can also provide insights into the effectiveness of your marketing channels. By tracking where your backers are coming from, you can determine which platforms or campaigns are driving the most conversions. For example, if you notice that a majority of your backers are coming from social media, you can allocate more resources to those platforms. Conversely, if a particular marketing channel is not performing well, you may decide to shift your focus elsewhere. By analyzing backer data, you can optimize your marketing efforts and ensure that you are reaching the right audience through the most effective channels.

Another important aspect of backer data is analyzing pledge levels and funding trends. Are there any specific pledge levels that are attracting the most support? Are there any trends in funding amounts over time? This information can help you tailor your rewards and pricing structure to better meet the needs and preferences of your backers. For example, if you notice that a particular reward tier is very popular, you may consider adding additional options at similar price points. By adjusting your rewards based on backer data, you can maximize your funding potential and keep backers excited about supporting your project.

In addition to analyzing the quantitative aspects of backer data, it's also important to gather qualitative feedback from your backers. Take the time to read and respond to comments, messages, and surveys from your backers. This feedback can provide valuable insights into their experience with your campaign and their expectations for the project. By actively listening to your backers and incorporating their feedback, you can create a sense of community and ownership around your project. This, in turn, will help maintain momentum and keep backers engaged throughout the campaign.

Harnessing backer data is a crucial step in maintaining momentum during the mid-campaign phase. By analyzing demographics, preferences, behaviors, and funding trends, you can make informed decisions and adjustments to your campaign strategy. This data-driven approach will help you attract new backers, optimize your marketing efforts, tailor your rewards, and create a sense of community around your project. So don't let the mid-campaign slump get you down. Dive into your backer data and use it to power through and keep the energy alive. The success of your Kickstarter campaign is within reach.

7 The Final Push: Closing Your Campaign Strong

As you enter the final days of your Kickstarter campaign, it's crucial to understand the importance of creating a sense of urgency. This urgency will not only help drive last-minute backers to support your project, but it will also motivate your existing backers to increase their pledges.

One of the main reasons urgency is important in the final days is that it creates a fear of missing out (FOMO) among potential backers. By emphasizing the limited time left in your campaign, you create a sense of scarcity that makes people feel compelled to take action before it's too late. This can be done through regular updates and reminders, countdowns, and highlighting the remaining funding goal to show how close you are to achieving it.

To effectively create urgency, it's important to leverage your existing backers and their enthusiasm for your project. Encourage them to share their support on social media and personal networks, urging others to back the campaign before it ends. Utilize testimonials and success stories from your current backers to showcase the positive impact your project has already made and why others should contribute. This social proof can help build trust and urgency among potential backers.

Another strategy to create urgency is to offer limited-time rewards or incentives exclusively for the final days of your campaign. This could include discounted prices, special editions of your product, or early access to certain features. By providing these time-sensitive offers, you give potential backers a reason to act now rather than waiting until later. It's important to communicate these limited-time rewards clearly and prominently on your Kickstarter page and through your campaign updates.

In addition to creating urgency, it's important to keep your backers engaged and informed during the final days. Regular updates are key to remind them of the campaign's progress, share any exciting developments or stretch goals achieved, and thank them for their support. This ongoing communication helps maintain a sense of excitement and urgency among your backers and encourages them to continue supporting and sharing your campaign.

As the final days of your campaign unfold, it's

crucial to keep a close eye on your progress and adjust your strategies accordingly. If you notice that your campaign is falling short of its funding goal, it's important to react quickly and pivot if necessary. Consider reaching out to your existing backers for their feedback and suggestions on how to generate more support. It's also worth exploring new marketing tactics such as reaching out to relevant influencers, hosting live Q&A sessions, or partnering with complementary projects for cross-promotion.

Understanding the importance of urgency in your Kickstarter's final days is vital for achieving a successful campaign. By creating a sense of scarcity, leveraging your existing backers, offering time-sensitive rewards, and maintaining regular communication, you can motivate last-minute backers and encourage them to support your project before time runs out. Remember to adapt your strategies based on the campaign's progress and always keep your backers engaged and informed. With the right tactics and a strong sense of urgency, you can make the most of your final days and achieve your fundraising goals.

Encouraging Last-Minute Backer Engagement Effectively

With the right strategies, you can effectively capture their attention and inspire them to contribute to your project. Here are some tips on how to encourage last-minute backer engagement effectively:

1. Communicate the Sense of Urgency: As mentioned earlier, creating a sense of urgency is vital in the final days of your campaign. Clearly communicate the remaining time left in your campaign and emphasize that it's the last chance for potential backers to get involved. Use countdowns, bold call-to-action statements, and visual reminders to make it clear that time is running out.

2. Highlight Progress and Milestones: Throughout your campaign, you should regularly update your backers on the progress you've made and any milestones achieved. In the final days, it's essential to showcase this progress and celebrate how far you've come. This will not only create excitement among your existing backers but also make potential backers feel more confident in supporting your project.

3. Utilize Backer Testimonials: Testimonials from your existing backers can be a powerful tool in convincing last-minute backers to contribute. Reach out to your backers and ask them to share

their experiences and thoughts about your project. Highlight these testimonials in your campaign updates, social media posts, and on your Kickstarter page. Seeing real people endorsing your project will help build trust and encourage others to back your campaign.

4. Leverage Social Media and Personal Networks: Your existing backers can play a significant role in promoting your campaign in its final days. Encourage them to share their support on social media and personal networks, urging others to back your project before time runs out. Offer incentives, such as shoutouts or exclusive rewards, to those who help spread the word. By tapping into the networks of your backers, you can reach a wider audience and increase your chances of attracting last-minute backers.

5. Offer Limited-Time Rewards: Incentivize last-minute backers by offering limited-time rewards or discounts exclusively for the final days of your campaign. This creates a sense of urgency and gives potential backers a reason to act now rather than later. Clearly communicate these limited-time offers on your Kickstarter page, in your campaign updates, and through your social media channels. Make it clear that these rewards will not be

available once the campaign ends, adding an extra incentive for potential backers to take action.

6. Maintain Regular Communication: In the final days of your campaign, it's crucial to keep your backers engaged and informed. Continue sending regular updates to remind them of the campaign's progress, share any exciting developments or stretch goals achieved, and thank them for their support. Regular communication not only maintains excitement and urgency among your existing backers but also reminds potential backers that your project is still active and needs their support.

7. Personalize Your Outreach: As the final days of your campaign unfold, consider reaching out to potential backers individually. Send personalized messages expressing your gratitude for their interest in your project and why their support would be invaluable. Tailor these messages based on their previous interactions with your campaign or their expressed interests. By showing genuine interest in their support, you can create a personal connection and motivate them to contribute.

By implementing these strategies, you can effectively encourage last-minute backer engagement and maximize your chances of reaching your fundraising goals. The final days of your Kickstarter campaign are an exciting time filled with potential, so make sure to give it your all and leave no stone unturned. Remember, every last-minute backer counts, and with the right approach, you can turn them into enthusiastic supporters of your project.

Strategies for Handling Unforeseen Challenges During Your Campaign

Despite your best planning and preparation, you may still encounter unexpected hurdles along the way. It's essential to have strategies in place to handle these unforeseen challenges and ensure the success of your campaign.

1. Stay Calm and Assess the Situation: When faced with an unexpected challenge, the first step is to stay calm and assess the situation objectively. Panicking or becoming overwhelmed will only hinder your ability to find a solution. Take a step back, gather all the relevant information, and analyze the problem from different angles.

2. Communicate Transparently with Your Backers: Open and honest communication is crucial when addressing unforeseen challenges during your campaign. Your backers are investing their trust and money in your project, and they deserve to be

kept informed. Provide regular updates, explaining the situation, and the steps you're taking to resolve the issue. By being transparent, you'll build trust and maintain your backers' support.

3. Seek Expert Advice or Consultation: Depending on the nature of the challenge, it may be beneficial to seek expert advice or consultation. Whether it's legal, technical, or logistical expertise, reaching out to professionals who can provide guidance can help you navigate through the obstacle. Don't hesitate to ask for help when needed.

4. Pivot and Adapt: One of the hallmarks of successful entrepreneurs is their ability to pivot and adapt in the face of challenges. If a particular strategy or aspect of your campaign isn't working as planned, be open to adjusting your approach. Consider alternative solutions and explore new avenues that can help overcome the challenge. By being flexible, you can turn setbacks into opportunities.

5. Rally Your Community for Support: Your backers and the wider community that has rallied behind your project can be an invaluable source of support when facing unexpected challenges. Reach out to them for assistance, whether it's in the form of advice, suggestions, or resources. Your community

has already shown their belief in your project, and they will likely be willing to help you overcome any hurdles that come your way.

6. Prioritize and Focus: Unforeseen challenges can be overwhelming, and it's easy to feel scattered or lose sight of your goals. Take a step back and prioritize the most critical aspects that need immediate attention. By focusing your efforts on the most crucial areas, you can effectively tackle the challenge at hand without wasting time or resources.

7. Stay Positive and Learn from the Experience: Remember that setbacks and challenges are part of the journey towards success. Instead of getting discouraged, embrace the challenge as an opportunity to learn and grow. By maintaining a positive mindset, you'll be better equipped to find creative solutions and bounce back stronger than before.

Handling unforeseen challenges during your Kickstarter campaign can be stressful, but with the right strategies and mindset, you can overcome them successfully. Stay calm, communicate transparently with your backers, seek expert advice when needed, be willing to adapt, rally your community for support, prioritize and focus on the most critical aspects, and maintain a positive outlook throughout the process. By doing so, you'll be well-prepared to tackle any unexpected hurdles and ensure the long-term success of your campaign. Remember, challenges are opportunities in disguise – embrace them and keep pushing forward towards your goals.

Setting Yourself Up for Success Post-Campaign

Now, it's time to set yourself up for long-term success after the campaign concludes. In this section, we'll explore strategies to help you navigate the post-campaign phase and ensure a smooth transition into the next steps of your project.

1. Fulfillment Planning:

The first and most crucial step after your Kickstarter campaign is to develop a comprehensive fulfillment plan. This plan outlines how you'll deliver rewards to your backers, ensuring their satisfaction and maintaining your reputation. Start by organizing all the necessary information, including backer details, reward choices, and shipping addresses. Next, establish a timeline for production, packaging, and shipping. Be realistic about your capacity and allocate resources accordingly. Communicate your fulfillment plan with your backers, keeping them informed about the progress and estimated delivery dates. By being transparent and proactive in your communication, you'll build trust and maintain the excitement surrounding your project.

2. Manufacturing and Production:

Depending on the nature of your project, manufacturing and production might be a critical step post-campaign. If you're creating a physical product, ensure that you have all the necessary resources, suppliers, and manufacturing partners lined up. Communicate with them regularly to ensure a smooth production process. Pay attention to quality control, packaging, and any potential delays that may arise. Be prepared to make adjustments and keep your backers informed of any changes in the production timeline. By staying on top of manufacturing and production, you'll be able to deliver high-quality rewards that meet your backers' expectations.

3. Backer Communication:

Throughout the post-campaign phase, maintaining open lines of communication with your backers is crucial. Provide regular updates on the progress of your project, manufacturing milestones, and any challenges you encounter along the way. Be transparent about any delays or setbacks, and reassure your backers that their support is valued and appreciated. By keeping them informed, you'll not only build trust but also maintain their enthusiasm and engagement for your project. Utilize platforms such as email newsletters, social media, and Kickstarter updates to communicate effectively with your backers.

4. Building a Community:

Beyond the Kickstarter campaign, it's essential to focus on building a strong community around your project. Your backers are more than just financial supporters; they are potential brand ambassadors who can help you reach a wider audience. Engage with your community by hosting virtual events, offering exclusive perks or discounts, and soliciting feedback on future product developments. Encourage your backers to share their experiences with your project on social media and leave reviews on relevant platforms. By nurturing a supportive and engaged community, you'll create a lasting network of supporters who will champion your project and future endeavors.

5. Marketing and Promotion:

Even after your Kickstarter campaign ends,

marketing and promotion should remain a priority. Take advantage of the momentum generated during your campaign and continue to promote your project through various channels. Utilize social media platforms, blogs, podcasts, and relevant online communities to raise awareness and attract new customers. Consider reaching out to influencers, bloggers, and media outlets to showcase your project and its success. By maintaining a consistent marketing strategy, you'll continue to generate interest and support for your project long after the Kickstarter campaign has ended.

6. Learning and Growth:

Finally, take the time to reflect on your Kickstarter campaign and learn from the experience. Evaluate what worked well and what could have been improved. Seek feedback from your backers and take their suggestions into account. Use this information to refine your approach and make informed decisions for future projects. The journey doesn't end with one successful campaign; it's an ongoing process of learning, growth, and innovation. By embracing the lessons learned and adapting your strategies, you'll be well-equipped to achieve even greater success in the future.

8 Post-Campaign: Fulfillment and Beyond

As you embark on the next phase of bringing your project to life, it's important to take a moment to celebrate and reflect on the journey you've been on.

Think back to the very beginning, when the idea for your project first sparked in your mind. You had a vision, a dream, and through the power of crowdfunding, you were able to turn that dream into a reality. Remember the excitement and anticipation as you launched your campaign, sharing your passion with the world and hoping that others would believe in it too.

Then came the nail-biting days and weeks of the campaign itself. You watched as the numbers ticked up, inching closer and closer to your funding goal. You felt a mix of nervousness and exhilaration as each new backer pledged their support. And finally, that incredible moment when you reached your goal, and maybe even exceeded it. The feeling of joy and accomplishment is one that you'll never forget.

But the campaign journey wasn't just about the numbers. It was about the connections you made along the way. The messages of encouragement from friends, family, and strangers who believed in your project. The community that rallied behind you, sharing your campaign with their own networks, and helping to spread the word. It was a journey of collaboration and support, and it's important to remember and appreciate all the people who played a role in your success.

Take a moment to think about all the hard work that went into making your campaign a reality. The late nights spent crafting the perfect pitch video, the countless revisions of your project description, and the meticulous planning of rewards and stretch goals. It wasn't always easy, but you persevered and it paid off.

Now, as you move into the next phase of your project, it's important to carry this sense of celebration and gratitude with you. Your backers believed in you and your project, and they deserve to be part of the journey moving forward. Show your appreciation by keeping them updated on the progress of your project, sharing behind-the-scenes peeks, and involving them in decision-making whenever possible. Let them know that their support wasn't just for the campaign, but for the long-term success of your project.

So take a moment to celebrate. You've come a long way, and you've achieved something truly remarkable. But remember, this is just the beginning. The real work is yet to come, and with the support of your backers and the community you've built, there's no limit to what you can accomplish. Keep moving forward, stay passionate, and continue to share your journey with the world.

Navigating the Murky Waters of Post-Campaign Production Challenges

Your project is now fully funded, and you are one step closer to turning your dream into a reality. However, now comes the challenging part - navigating the murky waters of post-campaign production.

While running a Kickstarter campaign is exciting, fulfilling the promises you made to your backers can be a daunting task. Production challenges can arise, causing delays and unexpected hurdles along the way. It's important to be prepared and have a plan in place to handle these challenges effectively.

The first step in navigating these murky waters is to assess the scope of your project and identify potential production challenges. Take the time to thoroughly review your project plan and make note of any potential roadblocks that may arise during production. Are there any specific components or materials that may be difficult to source? Are there any manufacturing processes that may take longer than anticipated? By identifying these potential challenges early on, you can develop contingency plans and mitigate any potential delays.

Next, communicate with your suppliers and manufacturing partners. It's crucial to establish open lines of communication with all the parties involved in your project's production. Regularly check in with them to ensure that everything is on track and to address any concerns or issues that may arise. Be transparent with your backers about any potential delays and keep them informed every step of the way. By keeping them in the loop, they will feel involved and understand the challenges you are facing.

Flexibility is key when it comes to navigating post-campaign production challenges. It's important to be adaptable and willing to adjust your plans as needed. Sometimes, unforeseen circumstances may require you to change suppliers or modify certain aspects of your project. While it may be disappointing, remember that the end goal is to deliver a high-quality product to your backers. Keep an open mind and explore alternative options if necessary.

Another important aspect of navigating production challenges is managing your own expectations. It's natural to want to deliver your project as quickly as possible, but it's important to prioritize quality over speed. Rushing production can lead to mistakes and compromise the overall quality of your product. Remember that your backers are eagerly awaiting their rewards, and they will appreciate a well-crafted and thoughtfully produced item, even if it takes a little longer.

Finally, lean on your support network. Don't be afraid to reach out to fellow project creators, industry experts, and your Kickstarter community for advice and support. They have likely faced similar challenges and can offer valuable insights and guidance. Building a network of like-minded individuals who can share their experiences and knowledge can be invaluable in navigating post-campaign production challenges.

How to Manage Your Backer's Expectations After a Successful Campaign

Here are some key steps to effectively manage

your backer's expectations after a successful campaign:

1. Be Transparent and Communicate Regularly: Open and honest communication is crucial in keeping your backers informed and engaged. Regularly update them on the progress of your project, including any potential delays or challenges you may be facing. By keeping them in the loop, they will appreciate your transparency and understand the realities of bringing a project to life.

2. Set Realistic Timelines: While it's tempting to promise quick delivery to your backers, it's important to set realistic timelines based on the complexity of your project and any potential production challenges. Be transparent about the estimated delivery dates and communicate any changes or delays that may occur along the way. Your backers will appreciate the honesty and understanding that delays are often beyond your control.

3. Provide Detailed Updates: In addition to regular communication, provide detailed updates on the progress of your project. Share photos, videos, and behind-the-scenes peeks to keep your backers engaged and excited about the development of your project. By involving them in the journey, they

will feel more connected to your project and the fulfillment process.

4. Address Concerns Promptly: As you communicate with your backers, be prepared to address any concerns or questions they may have. Respond to inquiries in a timely manner and provide helpful and informative answers. By being responsive and attentive to their needs, you will foster a sense of trust and satisfaction among your backers.

5. Quality Assurance: One of the most important aspects of managing backer's expectations is ensuring that the final product meets or exceeds their expectations. Conduct thorough quality checks throughout the production process to ensure that the product is of the highest quality. If any issues or defects arise, communicate them to your backers and provide solutions to rectify the situation. By demonstrating your commitment to delivering a high-quality product, you will build trust and loyalty among your backers.

6. Surprise and Delight: To go above and beyond in managing your backer's expectations, consider adding a little something extra to their rewards. It could be a handwritten thank-you note, an exclusive update, or a small gift related to your

project. These thoughtful gestures will make your backers feel appreciated and valued, and they will be more likely to support your future endeavors.

Remember, managing your backer's expectations is an ongoing process that requires constant communication and transparency. By being open, honest, and responsive to their needs, you will not only ensure a successful fulfillment process but also build a loyal and engaged community around your project. So, keep your backers in the loop, address their concerns, and deliver a high-quality product that exceeds their expectations. With these strategies in place, you are on your way to maintaining the support and enthusiasm of your backers long after the campaign has ended.

Keeping Your Backers Informed and Engaged

Effective communication is the backbone of a successful post-campaign experience. It's not enough to simply update your backers sporadically or only when there are significant developments. To keep your backers informed and engaged, you must maintain a continuous stream of communication throughout the entire fulfillment process and beyond.

Consistent updates are key. Regularly share

progress updates, milestones reached, and any challenges or delays that may arise. This keeps your backers in the loop and shows them that their support is appreciated and valued. Whether it's a monthly email, a blog post, or social media updates, find a communication channel that works best for you and stick to a schedule.

But communication is a two-way street. It's not just about sharing information; it's about fostering a sense of community and engagement. Encourage your backers to ask questions, share their thoughts, and provide feedback. Respond promptly and thoughtfully to their inquiries, and consider hosting live Q&A sessions or AMAs (Ask Me Anything) to provide a more interactive and personal experience. By actively engaging with your backers, you make them feel like they are an integral part of your project's journey.

In addition to regular updates and interaction, it's important to provide behind-the-scenes peeks and exclusive content to your backers. Share photos or videos of your production process, sneak peeks of new features or designs, or exclusive updates on the development of your project. By giving your backers an insider's view, you make them feel like they are part of something special. This not only keeps them excited and engaged but also strengthens their connection to your project.

Consider utilizing project management tools or backer surveys to gather feedback and preferences from your backers. This allows them to have a voice in the development of your project and helps you tailor your communication and updates to their specific interests and needs. By actively involving your backers in decision-making, you create a sense of ownership and investment in your project's success.

Don't underestimate the power of expressing gratitude. Take the time to thank your backers for their support, whether it's through a personal email, a handwritten note, or a special update. Show them that their contributions have made a difference and that you appreciate their belief in your project. This small gesture goes a long way in fostering a positive and supportive community.

Finally, continue to communicate with your backers even after your project is fulfilled. Share updates on any future plans or developments, involve them in new projects or campaigns, and maintain an ongoing relationship. By nurturing this post-campaign community, you not only maintain their support but also increase the likelihood of future contributions and word-of-mouth recommendations.

Building a Thriving Post-Campaign Community: Making the Most of Your Success

Here are some strategies to make the most of your success and create a vibrant post-campaign community:

1. Foster a Sense of Belonging: Your backers are more than just financial supporters; they are now part of your project's journey. Make them feel like valued members of a community by creating a dedicated space for them to connect and engage. This could be a private forum, a social media group, or even a dedicated email newsletter. Encourage them to share their thoughts, ideas, and experiences related to your project. By fostering a sense of belonging, you'll create a loyal and engaged community.

2. Continue to Share Updates: Just because your project is funded doesn't mean you should stop providing updates to your backers. In fact, regular communication is key to maintaining their interest and involvement. Share behind-the-scenes updates, milestones achieved, and any new developments or plans for the future. By keeping your backers informed and involved, they will

continue to feel connected to your project and invested in its success.

3. Involve Your Backers in Decision-Making: Your backers are not just passive supporters; they have valuable insights and opinions. Consider involving them in decision-making processes, such as selecting new features, colors, or designs. Conduct surveys or polls to gather their feedback and preferences. By actively involving your backers, you make them feel like active participants in the project and increase their sense of ownership.

4. Offer Exclusive Benefits and Rewards: Show your appreciation to your backers by offering them exclusive benefits and rewards. This could include early access to new products, special discounts, or limited edition merchandise. By providing exclusive perks, you create a sense of exclusivity and make your backers feel like VIP members of your community.

5. Host Events and Meetups: Take your online community offline by organizing events and meetups where backers can connect with you and fellow supporters in person. This could be a launch party, a workshop, or a casual meetup. These face-to-face interactions will strengthen the bonds within your community and create lasting relationships.

6. Encourage User-Generated Content: Your backers are likely passionate about your project, so why not tap into their creativity? Encourage them to share user-generated content related to your project, such as photos, videos, or testimonials. This not only showcases their enthusiasm but also serves as social proof for potential new backers. Highlight and share their content on your website, social media channels, or newsletters to recognize and celebrate their contributions.

Building a thriving post-campaign community is an ongoing process that requires time and effort. By fostering a sense of belonging, maintaining open communication, and involving your backers in decision-making, you can create a vibrant community that will continue to support and champion your projects. Remember, your backers are more than just financial supporters; they are now your brand advocates and partners. Treat them with respect, engage with them regularly, and create opportunities for connection.

9 Legal and Financial Considerations

Kickstarter is an incredibly popular platform for crowdfunding, but it's important to fully understand its terms of use before launching your campaign. By familiarizing yourself with the key takeaways from Kickstarter's terms of use, you can ensure that your campaign stays within the legal boundaries and maximize your chances of success.

One of the first things to understand is that Kickstarter is not just a platform for selling products or services. It's a platform for creative projects. This means that your campaign should focus on a specific creative endeavor, whether it's developing a new gadget, creating a work of art, or producing a film. Keep in mind that Kickstarter is not the place to raise money for personal causes or charities.

Next, it's important to understand that Kickstarter operates on an "all-or-nothing" funding model. This means that if your campaign doesn't reach its funding goal within the specified timeframe, you won't receive any of the pledged funds. It's crucial to set a realistic funding goal that takes into account the costs associated with your project, as well as any fees or taxes that may be deducted from the funds raised.

When it comes to rewards for backers, Kickstarter requires that you deliver what you promise. If you offer a certain reward tier to backers, you must be able to fulfill that commitment. Failure to do so can lead to legal issues and damage your reputation. Make sure to carefully consider the logistics and costs associated with each reward tier before including it in your campaign.

Additionally, it's important to disclose all relevant information about your project in a transparent and honest manner. Kickstarter requires that you provide accurate and truthful information about your project, including any risks or challenges that may arise. Transparency is key to building trust with potential backers and maintaining a positive reputation on the platform.

Intellectual property is another important consideration when using Kickstarter. Before launching your campaign, it's crucial to ensure that your project does not infringe upon any existing copyrights, trademarks, or patents. This includes any music, images, or other creative elements used in your project. It's recommended to consult with a lawyer or intellectual property expert to ensure that your project is legally sound.

Finally, it's important to understand that Kickstarter is not responsible for the success or failure of your project. While the platform provides a valuable opportunity to reach a large audience and raise funds, the ultimate responsibility lies with you as the creator. This means that you must be proactive in promoting your campaign, engaging with backers, and delivering on your promises.

Safeguarding Your Big Idea: Protecting Your Intellectual Property

You've come up with a brilliant idea for a new product or creative project, and you're ready to bring it to life through a Kickstarter campaign. But before you launch your campaign and share your big idea with the world, it's important to take steps to protect your intellectual property.

Intellectual property refers to the legal rights that creators have over their inventions, designs, and creative works. It's crucial to safeguard your intellectual property to prevent others from copying or stealing your ideas. Here are some key strategies to consider:

First, it's important to conduct a thorough search to ensure that your idea or invention is original and does not infringe upon any existing patents, trademarks, or copyrights. This will help you avoid legal issues down the line and protect your project's unique features. You can perform a search on the United States Patent and Trademark Office (USPTO) website or consult with an intellectual property lawyer for professional advice.

Once you have determined that your idea is original, it's a good idea to file for a patent, trademark, or copyright to legally protect your intellectual property. A patent grants you exclusive rights to your invention, while a trademark protects your brand name, logo, or slogan. Copyrights, on the other hand, protect original works of authorship, such as music, art, or literature. Filing for these protections can be a complex and time-consuming process, so it's recommended to seek assistance from an intellectual property attorney.

Another important step in safeguarding your intellectual property is to maintain confidentiality. Before launching your Kickstarter campaign, consider requiring potential collaborators or partners to sign a non-disclosure agreement (NDA). An NDA is a legally binding contract that prevents parties from sharing or using confidential information without permission. By using NDAs, you can ensure that your idea remains protected while you explore partnerships or seek feedback on your project.

When it comes to sharing information about your project on your Kickstarter campaign page, be cautious about disclosing too much detail. While it's important to provide potential backers with enough information to generate interest and trust, be mindful of revealing trade secrets or sensitive information that could be exploited by competitors. Focus on showcasing the unique aspects of your project without giving away all the technical or design specifics.

In addition to these proactive steps, it's crucial to monitor and enforce your intellectual property rights. Keep an eye out for any instances of infringement, whether it's someone copying your product or using your brand name without permission. If you come across any unauthorized use of your intellectual property, consult with an intellectual property attorney to explore your legal options. Taking swift action can help protect your rights and maintain the value of your intellectual property.

Beyond Your Projected Budget: Preparing for

Unforeseen Costs

Launching a Kickstarter campaign can be an exciting way to bring your business idea to life and secure the funding you need. However, it's essential to prepare for the possibility of unforeseen costs that may arise during the course of your project. By understanding the importance of budgeting and preparing for unexpected expenses, you can ensure that your campaign stays on track and achieves the success you envision.

One of the most crucial aspects of preparing for unforeseen costs is to create a detailed budget from the outset. When setting your funding goal, it's important to factor in all the expenses associated with your project, including manufacturing costs, shipping and fulfillment, marketing and advertising, and any fees or taxes that may be deducted from the funds raised. By considering these expenses upfront, you can set a realistic funding goal that will cover all your project's needs.

It's also a good idea to build in a contingency fund within your budget. This will provide a buffer for any unexpected expenses that may arise during the course of your campaign. Unforeseen costs can include anything from unexpected manufacturing delays or equipment breakdowns to additional marketing expenses or the need for additional staff. By having a contingency fund in place, you can mitigate the financial impact of these unexpected costs and ensure that your project stays on track.

Another strategy for preparing for unforeseen costs is to research and understand any potential risks or challenges that may arise during your project. For example, if you are manufacturing a physical product, there may be delays in production or supply chain issues that could impact your timeline and budget. By identifying and understanding these risks upfront, you can be better prepared to handle them if they occur and adjust your budget accordingly.

In addition to budgeting and risk management, it's important to be proactive in monitoring your campaign's progress and expenses throughout the fundraising period. Regularly review your budget and compare it to the funds raised to ensure that you are on track and have enough funds to cover your expenses. If you notice any discrepancies or unexpected costs, it's essential to address them promptly and adjust your budget or fundraising strategy if necessary.

Crowdfunding platforms like Kickstarter also provide opportunities for you to communicate and engage with your backers. Use this opportunity to keep your backers informed about any changes or updates regarding your project's budget. Transparency is key when it comes to managing unforeseen costs. By communicating openly with your backers and keeping them informed, you can maintain their trust and support.

Finally, it's important to remember that even with careful budgeting and planning, unexpected costs can still arise. It's crucial to be adaptable and willing to make adjustments to your project if needed. This may include finding alternative suppliers, cutting back on certain expenses, or seeking additional funding sources. By being flexible and resourceful, you can navigate any unforeseen costs that come your way and keep your project moving forward.

Tax Implications of a Successful Kickstarter Campaign

Launching a successful Kickstarter campaign is an exciting accomplishment. It means that you have successfully engaged with your audience, gained their support, and raised the funds needed to bring your project to life. However, it's important to understand that with success comes responsibility, especially when it comes to the tax implications of a successful Kickstarter campaign.

While crowdfunding campaigns on platforms like Kickstarter are not considered traditional income, they are not completely exempt from taxation. The funds you raise through your campaign may be subject to certain tax obligations, depending on the specific circumstances of your project and your location. Here are some key tax considerations to keep in mind as you celebrate the success of your Kickstarter campaign:

1. Categorize your income correctly: When you receive funds through your Kickstarter campaign, it's important to correctly categorize them as either income or a non-taxable gift. The distinction depends on whether you are providing goods or services in return for the funds. If you are offering tangible goods, such as a product or artwork, the funds you receive are generally considered taxable income. On the other hand, if you are providing non-tangible rewards, such as early access or exclusive content, the funds may be considered a non-taxable gift. It's important to consult with a tax professional to ensure that you are categorizing your income correctly and reporting it accurately.

2. Keep track of your expenses: Throughout your Kickstarter campaign, you will incur various expenses related to the production and fulfillment

of your project. It's crucial to keep detailed records of these expenses, as they can be deducted from your overall income for tax purposes. Deductible expenses may include manufacturing costs, shipping fees, marketing and advertising expenses, fees paid to Kickstarter or other crowdfunding platforms, and any professional services you may have enlisted, such as legal or accounting assistance. By keeping track of your expenses, you can minimize your overall tax liability.

3. Understand sales tax obligations: Depending on the nature of your project and the goods or services you offer as rewards, you may be required to collect and remit sales tax to the appropriate taxing authorities. Sales tax obligations vary from state to state and even from country to country, so it's important to research and understand the specific regulations that apply to you. Failure to comply with sales tax obligations can result in penalties and legal consequences. Consult with a tax professional or seek guidance from your local taxing authority to ensure that you are meeting all applicable sales tax requirements.

4. Consult with a tax professional: Tax laws can be complex and vary depending on your location and specific circumstances. It's highly recommended to consult with a tax professional who specializes in

crowdfunding or small business taxation. A tax professional can help you navigate the intricacies of tax laws, identify any potential deductions or credits that may be available to you, and ensure that you are in compliance with all applicable tax obligations. While it may require an investment upfront, consulting with a tax professional can save you time, money, and potential headaches in the long run.

Launching a successful Kickstarter campaign is a significant achievement, but it's important to understand and fulfill your tax obligations. By properly categorizing your income, keeping track of expenses, understanding sales tax obligations, and consulting with a tax professional, you can celebrate your success responsibly and ensure that your Kickstarter campaign remains a positive and rewarding experience both legally and financially.

10 Analyzing the Steps to a Winning Kickstarter

When it comes to running a successful Kickstarter campaign, there are certain key elements that can make all the difference. By dissecting the strategies used by previous winners, we can uncover the secret ingredients that contribute to their success.

One of the most crucial factors is having a clear and compelling project concept. Successful campaigns often have a unique and innovative idea that captures the attention of potential backers. They offer something fresh and exciting, making it easy for people to see the value in supporting the project.

In addition to a strong concept, successful campaigns also have a well-thought-out and detailed plan. This includes a clear timeline for project completion, a breakdown of how the funds will be used, and a realistic budget. Backers want to see that you have carefully considered every aspect of your project and have a solid plan in place to ensure its success.

Another key element is effective communication. Successful campaigns engage with their backers regularly, keeping them updated on the progress of the project and addressing any concerns or questions they may have. This builds trust and confidence in the campaign, increasing the likelihood of continued support.

Moreover, successful campaigns know the importance of setting realistic funding goals. They take the time to research and understand the costs associated with their project, ensuring that their funding target accurately reflects what is needed to bring their idea to life. Over-ambitious goals can deter potential backers, so it is essential to strike the right balance between ambition and feasibility.

Furthermore, successful campaigns make smart use of social media and other marketing strategies to reach a wide audience. They leverage their networks, engage with influencers, and create compelling content to generate buzz and excitement around their project. They understand the power of storytelling and use it to connect with their audience on an emotional level, inspiring them to become backers and advocates for the campaign.

Another element that contributes to success is offering attractive rewards. Backers want to feel that they are getting something of value in return for their support, so it is crucial to create a range of enticing rewards that cater to different budgets and interests. The rewards should be unique, exclusive, and aligned with the project concept, making backers feel special and appreciated.

Finally, successful campaigns show gratitude and appreciation to their backers. They go above and beyond to acknowledge their support and make them feel like an integral part of the project. This includes personalized thank-you messages, regular updates on project progress, and even exclusive perks or bonuses for backers. By nurturing the relationship with their backers, successful campaigns build a loyal and supportive community that can help propel their project to new heights.

Unveiling the Secrets Behind Failed Kickstarter Projects: Lessons from Past Mistakes

Not every Kickstarter campaign ends in success. Many campaigns fall short of their funding goals and leave creators wondering what went wrong. In this section, we will delve into the secrets behind failed Kickstarter projects and learn valuable lessons from past mistakes.

One of the primary reasons for the failure of

Kickstarter campaigns is the lack of a compelling project concept. It's not enough to have a good idea; you need to present it in a way that captivates potential backers. Many failed campaigns failed to communicate their concept effectively, leaving potential supporters confused or uninterested. To avoid this pitfall, it is crucial to clearly articulate the unique selling point of your project and make it easy for people to understand its value.

Another common mistake made by unsuccessful campaigns is poor planning and lack of a detailed roadmap. Crowdfunding backers want to see that you have thought through all the aspects of your project and have a solid plan in place. Without a clear timeline, breakdown of how the funds will be used, and a realistic budget, backers may question your ability to deliver on your promises. It is essential to invest time in crafting a well-thought-out plan to instill confidence in potential backers.

Ineffective communication is another key factor that can lead to the downfall of a Kickstarter campaign. Lack of updates, delayed responses to backer inquiries, or simply failing to engage with your audience can create doubt and mistrust. Building a community around your campaign is crucial, and that starts with transparent and regular communication. By keeping backers informed about progress, addressing concerns promptly, and maintaining an open line of communication, you can foster trust and build a supportive network.

Setting unrealistic funding goals is a significant mistake that many failed campaigns make. While it's important to aim high and have ambitious goals, they need to be grounded in reality. Overestimating the amount of money needed can deter potential backers who may perceive the goal as unattainable. Conduct thorough research, assess your project's needs accurately, and set a funding target that aligns with your requirements.

Insufficient marketing and promotion efforts also contribute to the failure of many Kickstarter campaigns. A great idea alone is not enough; you need to create buzz and generate excitement around your project. Successful campaigns understand the power of leveraging social media and other marketing strategies to reach a wider audience. Building anticipation and showcasing the value of your project through compelling storytelling and engaging content can make all the difference in attracting backers.

Additionally, the rewards offered can make or break a Kickstarter campaign. Backers want to feel valued and appreciated, and offering lackluster or unattractive rewards can discourage potential supporters. Take the time to create a range of appealing rewards that align with your project and provide value to your backers. Personalization and exclusivity can go a long way in making your supporters feel special and appreciated.

Tips and Tricks for Your Kickstarter Campaign

Now that we have dissected successful and failed Kickstarter campaigns, it's time to translate these learnings into action. Here are some valuable tips and tricks to help you create a winning Kickstarter campaign of your own.

1. Start with a clear and compelling project concept: Your project concept is the foundation of your campaign, so make sure it is unique, innovative, and captures the attention of potential backers. Clearly articulate the value and benefits of your project to make it easy for people to understand why they should support you.

2. Plan, plan, plan: A well-thought-out and detailed plan is crucial for the success of your campaign. Develop a clear timeline for project completion, outline how the funds will be used, and create a realistic budget. Backers want to see that you have

considered every aspect of your project and have a solid plan in place.

3. Communicate effectively: Engage with your backers regularly and keep them updated on the progress of your project. Address any concerns or questions they may have promptly and transparently. Building trust and confidence in your campaign is essential, and effective communication is key to achieving this.

4. Set realistic funding goals: Do your research and understand the costs associated with your project. Set a funding target that accurately reflects what you need to bring your idea to life. Overestimating your funding goal can deter potential backers, so strike the right balance between ambition and feasibility.

5. Leverage social media and marketing strategies: Make use of social media platforms and other marketing strategies to reach a wider audience. Build anticipation and generate excitement around your project through compelling storytelling and engaging content. Create buzz and showcase the value of your project to attract backers.

6. Offer attractive rewards: Create a range of enticing rewards that cater to different budgets and

interests. Make sure the rewards are unique, exclusive, and aligned with your project concept. Your backers should feel that they are getting something of value in return for their support.

7. Show gratitude and appreciation: Thank your backers and make them feel like an integral part of your project. Personalized thank-you messages, regular updates on project progress, and exclusive perks or bonuses can go a long way in fostering a loyal and supportive community.

8. Learn from past mistakes: Study failed Kickstarter campaigns and understand the mistakes they made. Avoid common pitfalls such as a lack of a compelling project concept, poor planning, ineffective communication, setting unrealistic funding goals, insufficient marketing efforts, and unattractive rewards. By learning from these mistakes, you can increase your chances of success.

Case Studies Analysis: Learning From Real Life Successes and Failures

Case studies provide valuable insights into the real-life successes and failures of Kickstarter campaigns. By examining these case studies, we can learn from the experiences of others and apply those lessons to our own campaigns.

One example of a successful Kickstarter campaign is the Pebble Time smartwatch. This project aimed to create a smartwatch with an e-paper display and a long battery life. The campaign not only met its funding goal within minutes but also became the most funded project in Kickstarter history at the time. So, what made the Pebble Time campaign so successful?

Firstly, the creators had a clear and compelling project concept. They offered a unique product that stood out in the market, capturing the attention of potential backers. Additionally, they had a well-thought-out plan and communicated it effectively. They provided regular updates on the progress of the project, addressing any concerns or questions from backers promptly. This built trust and confidence in the campaign, encouraging continued support.

Another example of a successful Kickstarter campaign is the Coolest Cooler. This project aimed to create a multi-functional cooler with features like a blender, speakers, and USB chargers. The campaign raised over $13 million, making it one of the most successful Kickstarter projects ever. So, what were the key factors behind the success of the

Coolest Cooler campaign?

Similar to the Pebble Time campaign, the Coolest Cooler had a clear and compelling concept that appealed to potential backers. They also had a detailed plan and communicated it effectively, providing updates on project progress and engaging with their audience. Additionally, they leveraged social media and other marketing strategies to generate buzz and excitement around their project. This created a sense of anticipation and attracted a wide audience of backers.

Now let's look at some examples of failed Kickstarter campaigns and the lessons we can learn from them. One such example is the Zano drone project. This campaign aimed to create a palm-sized drone with advanced features. However, it ended up being one of the most high-profile failures on Kickstarter. So, what went wrong?

One of the main reasons for the failure of the Zano drone campaign was a lack of effective communication. The creators failed to provide regular updates and address concerns from backers promptly. This created doubt and mistrust, leading to a significant decline in support. Additionally, the campaign set an unrealistic funding goal, which made it seem unattainable to potential backers. This deterred support and ultimately led to the project's failure.

Another example of a failed Kickstarter campaign is the Asylum Playing Cards project. This campaign aimed to create a unique deck of playing cards with a horror theme. However, despite having a visually appealing concept, the campaign failed to generate enough interest and funding. So, what can we learn from this failure?

One key lesson from the Asylum Playing Cards campaign is the importance of effective marketing and promotion. The creators failed to leverage social media and other marketing strategies to reach a wider audience and generate excitement around their project. Without adequate promotion, the campaign struggled to attract enough backers. Additionally, the rewards offered were not attractive enough to entice potential supporters, leading to a lack of interest in the project.

Analyzing real-life successes and failures can provide valuable lessons for creating a winning Kickstarter campaign. By studying the strategies used by successful projects and the mistakes made by failed campaigns, we can gain insights into the key elements that contribute to success. Clear and compelling project concepts, detailed plans, effective communication, realistic funding goals, strategic marketing, attractive rewards, and gratitude towards backers are all essential factors for a successful Kickstarter campaign. So, take these lessons and apply them to your own campaign, increasing your chances of reaching your funding goals and turning your dreams into a reality.

Appendix

Tools and Resources

Before you launch, it's crucial to have all the essential tools in your arsenal for a successful pre-launch preparation. These tools will help you plan, organize, and optimize your campaign, ensuring that you start off on the right foot and attract backers from the get-go.

First and foremost, you need a platform to host your campaign. Kickstarter itself is the obvious choice, with its vast audience of potential backers and its reputation as one of the most popular crowdfunding platforms. Setting up your project on Kickstarter is relatively easy, and they provide a step-by-step guide to walk you through the process.

To effectively manage your campaign and keep track of all the moving parts, project management tools like Trello or Asana are essential. These platforms allow you to create and assign tasks, set deadlines, and collaborate with your team members. They provide a centralized hub for all your campaign-related activities, ensuring that nothing falls through the cracks.

In addition to project management tools, you'll also need a comprehensive spreadsheet to keep track of your budget, expenses, and backer rewards. Google Sheets or Microsoft Excel are both excellent options for creating and maintaining a detailed campaign finance tracker. Make sure to include columns for your funding goal, production costs, shipping expenses, and any other relevant financial information. This spreadsheet will serve as your financial compass throughout the campaign, helping you stay on track and make informed decisions.

Next, you'll need a reliable email marketing platform to communicate with your backers and potential supporters. Mailchimp and ConvertKit are popular options that allow you to create and automate email campaigns, segment your audience, and track the success of your emails. These platforms also provide customizable templates, making it easy to design professional-looking newsletters and updates.

Social media plays a crucial role in promoting your campaign and reaching a wider audience. Tools like Hootsuite or Buffer can help you manage and schedule your social media posts across multiple platforms, ensuring that you have a consistent and engaging presence online. These platforms also provide analytics to track the performance of your social media campaigns, allowing you to adjust your strategy accordingly.

To create eye-catching graphics and visuals for your campaign, design tools like Canva or Adobe Creative Cloud are indispensable. Canva is a user-friendly platform that offers a wide range of templates and design elements, allowing you to create stunning visuals even if you have no design experience. Adobe Creative Cloud, on the other hand, is a professional-grade suite of design software that provides more advanced features and flexibility.

Another crucial aspect of pre-launch preparation is conducting thorough market research. Tools like Google Trends and Google Keyword Planner can help you identify popular trends and search terms related to your product or industry. By understanding what your target audience is searching for, you can tailor your campaign messaging and keywords to maximize your visibility and attract the right backers.

Lastly, it's essential to have a comprehensive customer relationship management (CRM) system in place to manage your backers' information and communicate effectively. Tools like HubSpot or Zoho CRM allow you to track and organize your interactions with backers, store important contact details, and automate certain tasks like sending thank-you emails or follow-up surveys. A robust CRM system ensures that you can provide personalized and timely communication to your backers, enhancing their overall experience and increasing the likelihood of their continued support.

By utilizing these essential tools for pre-launch preparation, you'll be well-equipped to navigate the complexities of Kickstarter and launch a successful campaign. Remember, preparation is key, and investing time and effort into the planning phase will significantly increase your chances of reaching your funding goals. So, take advantage of these tools, streamline your processes, and get ready to launch a campaign that will capture the attention and support of backers worldwide.

Top Resource Platforms for Funding Support

Now that you have your pre-launch preparation in order, it's time to explore the top resource platforms that can provide additional support and funding for your Kickstarter campaign. These platforms offer various services and opportunities to connect with backers, investors, and mentors who can help take your campaign to the next level.

BackerClub is an exclusive community of experienced Kickstarter backers who support projects they find interesting. By joining BackerClub, you can gain access to a network of potential backers who are actively looking for innovative projects to support. This platform allows you to showcase your campaign to a targeted audience, increasing your chances of attracting high-quality backers who are likely to contribute significant amounts.

BackerKit is a project management and fulfillment platform that helps you streamline your post-campaign processes. With BackerKit, you can easily manage backer information, send surveys, and handle the fulfillment of rewards. This platform also provides advanced analytics and reporting features to help you understand your backers' preferences and improve future campaigns. BackerKit can be a valuable resource for managing your campaign's fulfillment process efficiently.

Funded Today is a crowdfunding agency that specializes in helping campaigns achieve their funding goals. They offer various services, including strategic consulting, video production, social media marketing, and PR outreach. Funded Today has a proven track record of helping campaigns raise millions of dollars, and their expertise can significantly boost your chances of success. Keep in mind that working with an agency like Funded Today may require an investment, but the potential return can be well worth it.

If you're looking to continue funding your project even after your Kickstarter campaign has ended, Indiegogo InDemand is a fantastic option. InDemand allows you to keep raising funds and accepting pre-orders for your product or project. This platform has a large user base and can provide exposure to a wider audience beyond your initial Kickstarter backers. Indiegogo InDemand can be a powerful tool for generating ongoing support and sales even after your initial campaign has ended.

If you're seeking more substantial investment opportunities, Crowdfunder is the platform for you. Crowdfunder connects startups and entrepreneurs with accredited investors who are looking to fund promising projects. Through Crowdfunder, you can create a campaign that showcases your business or product, and potentially attract investors who can provide the funding and expertise you need to grow your venture. Crowdfunder is an excellent resource for those looking to take their project to the next level with significant investment.

For filmmakers and creators in the entertainment industry, Seed&Spark offers a unique platform that focuses on supporting independent projects. This crowdfunding platform provides resources and tools specifically tailored for filmmakers, including funding opportunities, distribution support, and access to industry mentors. Seed&Spark can be an invaluable resource for filmmakers looking to gain exposure, secure funding, and navigate the complex landscape of the entertainment industry.

If you're looking for ongoing support for your creative work, Patreon is an excellent platform to consider. Patreon allows creators to receive recurring payments from their fans in exchange for exclusive content or perks. This platform enables you to build a community of dedicated supporters who believe in your work and are willing to provide continuous financial support. Whether you're a musician, artist, writer, or content creator, Patreon can provide a stable income stream that allows you to focus on creating your best work.

AngelList is a platform that connects startups with angel investors and venture capitalists. It's a powerful resource for entrepreneurs looking to secure substantial investment for their projects. AngelList provides a space to showcase your business, connect with potential investors, and receive funding and support to help your project thrive. If you have a tech or innovative startup, AngelList can be an invaluable resource for funding and networking opportunities.

These resource platforms can provide additional funding, support, and exposure to help take your Kickstarter campaign to new heights. Whether you're looking for targeted backers, fulfillment solutions, investment opportunities, or ongoing support, these platforms offer a range of options to suit your needs. Remember, crowdfunding success is not just about launching a campaign; it's about leveraging all available resources to maximize your chances of reaching your funding goals. So explore these platforms, seize the opportunities they offer, and make your crowdfunding dreams a reality.

Glossary

If you're new to the world of Kickstarter, you may find yourself overwhelmed by all the unfamiliar terminology and jargon used on the platform. But fear not, because in this section, we will decode all the key terms that every backer should know.

1. Backer: A backer is an individual or organization that supports a Kickstarter campaign by pledging a certain amount of money. Backers are essential to the success of a campaign, as their financial contributions help creators bring their ideas to life.

2. Pledge: When you decide to support a campaign, you make a pledge. This is the amount of money you are willing to contribute to the project. Pledges can vary from a few dollars to hundreds or even thousands, depending on your level of interest and the rewards offered by the creator.

3. Reward: One of the perks of backing a Kickstarter campaign is receiving rewards. These are incentives that creators offer to backers in exchange for their support. Rewards can range from exclusive merchandise, early access to products, or even a chance to be involved in the creative process.

4. Stretch Goal: Stretch goals are additional targets that creators set for their campaign once the initial funding goal has been reached. They are a way to incentivize backers to contribute more and can include added features, upgrades, or additional content. Stretch goals can help a campaign gain momentum and surpass its original funding target.

5. Early Bird: Many campaigns offer early bird rewards as a way to incentivize early backers. These are exclusive rewards or discounts that are available to those who pledge their support during the early stages of the campaign. Early bird rewards are often limited in quantity or time, so backers have to act quickly to take advantage of these special offers.

6. Funding Goal: The funding goal is the amount of money a creator needs to raise in order to bring their project to life. It includes the costs of production, manufacturing, and any other expenses associated with the project. It is important for creators to set a realistic funding goal that is achievable within the campaign's duration.

7. All-or-Nothing: Kickstarter operates on an all-or-nothing funding model, meaning that a campaign must reach its funding goal in order to receive any money at all. If the campaign falls short of its goal,

no money is collected from backers, and the project is not funded. This model is designed to minimize risks for backers and ensure that creators have the necessary resources to fulfill their promises.

8. Creator: The creator is the individual or team behind the Kickstarter campaign. They are responsible for bringing the project to life, fulfilling the rewards, and maintaining communication with their backers. Creators play a crucial role in building trust and keeping their backers updated throughout the campaign and beyond.

9. Campaign Duration: The campaign duration is the length of time that a creator sets for their Kickstarter campaign. It can vary from a few days to several weeks, depending on the complexity of the project and the funding goal. Creators need to carefully consider the duration to allow enough time to reach their target while also creating a sense of urgency for potential backers.

10. Update: Updates are important communications from creators to their backers throughout the campaign. They provide progress reports, announce new stretch goals or rewards, and keep backers informed about any changes or developments. Updates are a way to build a relationship with backers and create a sense of

community around the project.

Now that you have a solid understanding of these key terms, you are well-equipped to navigate the world of Kickstarter campaigns. Whether you're a backer or a creator, having a grasp of these terms will make the crowdfunding experience much smoother and more enjoyable. So go forth and explore the incredible projects on Kickstarter, and who knows, maybe your next big idea will become a reality with the support of the Kickstarter community.